Reviews of .

"*Deadly Equines* is a thought-provoking and challenging insight into an aspect of equine nature that we are perhaps unwilling to connect with, or even acknowledge. Through diligent historical research and eye witness accounts, O'Reilly, in his inimitable fashion, piques our curiosity and forces us to consider the possibility that the pony in our paddock could be harbouring a darker secret than we care to imagine. The central hypothesis of this work will make uncomfortable reading for those who perpetuate the cosy world of the horse as victim, prey and obedient herbivore. Yet it does more than this; it does not, I would argue, cause us to question the validity of the human equine relationship, it strengthens it, by showing us what a truly resilient and adaptable animal the horse really is. If you own a horse you should read this book, it may make you see him in a different light."
Garry Ashton-Coulton - Art Editor, *Horse* magazine, London.

"In his latest book, *Deadly Equines*, the renowned expert CuChullaine O'Reilly has investigated the carnivorous diet and predatory nature of horses. Supported by sources both ancient and modern, the volume provides material from film, the personal experience of noted explorers and evidence from veterinarians and anthropologists that the horse as herbivore is a matter of conditioning, not necessarily preference. This research provides the opportunity to rethink the relationship of humans and horses and the animal's natural behaviour in the environment. From habit and prejudice, humans have held outdated opinions about domesticated animals without any attempt to uncover their real inclinations. This research offers startling and revelatory insight about equines that appears irrefutable."
Dr. Ruth Carter - Professor of International Studies at Georgia College and State University.

"*Deadly Equines* describes some truly terrifying encounters that will not make easy reading for horse lovers. Few could fail to be horrified by the Man-eater of Lucknow and accounts of other homicidal horses. Such dramas aside, O'Reilly pulls together what is almost certainly the first serious piece of research into meat-eating equines, from the workhorses used to explore the Poles to cultures that trained their mounts to eat flesh. O'Reilly controversially suggests that many modern-day horse lovers have a sanitised view of the horse and suggests past generations may well have had a better understanding of their nature. His book offers an intriguing view of a largely unexplored part of equine history."

Neil Clarkson - Publisher of *Horse Talk* international equestrian news service.

"*Deadly Equines'* investigation of the of the O'Reilly Anomaly – i.e. the historical recurrence of omnivorous horses – makes for compelling reading. The various eye-witness testimonies across time and continents, many of them evidently reliable, constitute a particularly strong argument that more research seems warranted on this subject by equine biologists and zoologists."

Dr. David R. Dorondo - Department of History, Western Carolina University and author of *Riders of the Apocalypse: German Cavalry and Modern Warfare.*

"*Deadly Equines* is a wonderfully crafted, thought-provoking resource with a wide selection of horse myth, quotes and historical eye-witness accounts. The author's attention to the source material provides a more empirical look at lost fragments of horse lore and culture that have been either buried or dismissed as nothing more than scary fairy tales to regale your children with. Either way the book begs a renewed interest in and re-examination of the nature of the horse."

Diane Dowling - Director of the equestrian documentary *Of Horse & Man.*

"What a fantastic story! O'Reilly has gathered an astonishing amount of material to prove his thesis and clearly there is a message here which has been suppressed over the years. Everyone who associates with horses should read this book and

understand that there is much more to our relationship with these wonderful animals than has been previously understood."
Robin Hanbury-Tenison OBE - Long Rider and author of *The Oxford Book of Exploration.*

"*Deadly Equines* was riveting! It contains a vast collection of empirical evidence, meticulously researched, cross checked and collated into a gripping series of events that proves the existence of meat-eating horses throughout history. From historical texts to astounding pictorial evidence we are confronted with an aspect of the nature of the horse which has never before been brought to light. A must-read for all horse lovers."
Dr. Wendy Hofstee - Long Rider FRGS and BVSc MRCVS.

"*Deadly Equines* brings to light a rarely, if ever, discussed aspect of equine behaviour in a fascinating and informative way. Most readers are only familiar with highly romanticized accounts of horses, save for academic readers, and even 'bad horses' are generally discussed in a manner which is romantic. With this book, we're reminded that the animal world is much more intricate, and interesting, than myth suggests and that one of our oldest animal associates, the horse, is a more complex animal than we really know, even now."
Patrick Holscher - Society of the Military Horse.

"*Deadly Equines* is an extraordinary study and an intriguing account. This salutary read will provoke other observations regarding the O'Reilly Anomaly. For example, I'd been told about a chap in the Household Cavalry whose horse used to kill and eat pigeons."
Jeremy James - Long Rider FRGS and author of *The Byerley Turk.*

"*Deadly Equines* is a fascinating and utterly engrossing study that presents startling and convincing evidence for the carnivorous, or at least omnivorous, nature of horses. O'Reilly, founder of the Long Riders' Guild and a world-renowned expert on horses, has assembled an impressive body of evidence throughout history

and across the world of horses engaging in predatory-like behaviour and eating meat. This iconoclastic book shatters many cherished assumptions about horses and behaviour. It is an essential read for anyone with an interest in horses and should stimulate more research into this astonishing but neglected side of equine history. I highly recommend it".
Douglas Preston - Long Rider FRGS and author of *Cities of Gold*.

"*Deadly Equines* depicts a fascinating and barely known aspect of polar exploration history."
The Honourable Alexandra Shackleton - President of the James Caird Society

"Once again, CuChullaine O'Reilly has blown off the barn doors to reveal a fascinating and largely forgotten body of equestrian history that would suggest that the horse we think we know is instead a complex animal with behaviours that would puzzle, shock, and mortify modern horse owners. In his latest book, *Deadly Equines*, O'Reilly has uncovered and re-examined the historical evidence of the horse to reveal an animal capable of eating meat and killing for meat. This startling information will terrify the little girl with unicorns on her bedroom wall, but for those of us who own and live with horses, this information is fascinating and compelling, and will change the way you perceive the horse forever. With relentless research, numerous eyewitness accounts, and literary clues, O'Reilly has put together a body of evidence on meat-eating horses that should have encyclopaedia editors all over the world scrambling to re-edit their chapter on the horse."
Geoff Young - Publisher/Editor, *Horse Connection* magazine.

Deadly Equines

The Shocking True Story
of Meat-Eating
and Murderous Horses

by

CuChullaine O'Reilly FRGS

The Long Riders' Guild Press

www.classictravelbooks.com
www.horsetravelbooks.com
www.lrgaf.org

ISBN: 1-59048-003-1

Cover design by Brian Rooney, R7Media (www.r7media.com)

Dedicated to the memory of
Charles Darwin,
Historical Long Rider
and Scientific Explorer

"The most erroneous stories are those we think we know best - and therefore never scrutinize or question."

Professor Stephen Jay Gould

Introduction

I had no intention of straying down this road.

For the past ten years I have been actively gathering material from around the world, so as to complete the most extensive study of equestrian travel. This project was well under way when I came face to face with a mystery whose existence I had long avoided either investigating or revealing.

While composing the forthcoming Horse Travel Handbook, I was required to disclose the various ways and means by which diverse mounted cultures had successfully fed their horses in the past. I knew that lurking within my immense pile of notes, documents, rare books and interviews was information of a startling, some might say dreadful, nature.

Contrary to popular belief which states that horses are passive herbivores, as the Founder of the Long Riders Guild Academic Foundation (LRG-AF) I had repeatedly uncovered evidence indicating that horses were capable of eating meat. Running alongside that discovery was associated information proving that throughout history horses had savagely slain humans. As a lifelong horseman, part of my mind did not want to deal with this enigma, so it sat quietly ticking away like an equestrian bomb, while I postponed, procrastinated, and looked the other way.

Eventually the day came when I could not proceed with the Handbook until I had resolved the issue of what man had fed horses. That is how I took the reluctant decision to study systematically all the evidence I had found to date.

When I began this project, I believed I had a grasp of the basic premise. Actually I was woefully in the dark. What I had uncovered to date was only the tip of an equine iceberg. Thereafter I entered into the darkest part of the equestrian universe.

Originally I had learned about the meat-eating horses of Tibet and found a few tales regarding the activities of deadly horses which resided in various parts of the world. Armed with that original research, I sought out other evidence. It wasn't hard to find. Various sources of corroborating data, including legends, literature, cinema, news stories, scientific reports and eyewitness accounts were awaiting investigation.

www.lrgaf.org

None of these items had been hidden. They had instead been ignored, misunderstood or, in some cases, censored.

The more I discovered, the more obvious it became that the modern horse world had lost touch with an alarming type of equestrian wisdom which until recently had been common knowledge. Documents proved that previous generations had been fully aware of how dangerous horses could be, not to mention the fact that they were at times eager meat-eaters.

When I had completed gathering the data, I was stunned to realize that mankind had known about meat-eating horses for at least four thousand years, that horses had been known to consume nearly two dozen different types of protein, including human flesh, and that these episodes had occurred on every continent, including Antarctica. This wasn't an odd example or two, this amounted to a hidden history of horses.

Even more shocking was the realization that horses had perpetrated attacks which defied description and belief. These accounts included stories about eager man-killers, a stallion that terrorized an entire city and a "demon" horse who slew dozens but was later worshipped as a demigod.

Much of the material was highly disturbing and it certainly did not belong in the Horse Travel Handbook. It would have all remained academic, if I had not also uncovered recent news stories proving that this sort of lethal equine behaviour was responsible for the recent death of other humans, including at least one infant. Clearly, horses were still capable of homicidal rage and dietary deviance.

If these consistent truths about horses had been important enough for our ancestors to record, then, having learned of the child's death, I reasoned that I should alert the public to my findings.

First I shared my original work with other Long Riders, explorers and academics. Though they too were initially shocked, further discussion revealed unexpected similarities which linked various pieces of evidence. For example, not only had horses repeatedly slain predators such as lions, wolves and tigers in the past, they were still doing so today.

This collective research was dubbed "the O'Reilly Anomaly" during the time I was working on it, not out of any desire for recognition, but because the original nickname, "meat-eaters," was found to describe only half of the research. Thus the book consists of two threads: episodes involving meat-eating equines and incidents wherein horses slew other mammals, including human beings. They are deliberately interwoven, so as to allow the reader to study simultaneously mankind's 30,000 year link to the horse.

Despite my best efforts to keep the material as objective and emotionally low-key as possible, much of this book will still prove to be highly disturbing. This is because there are terrible tales within which have haunted mankind's dreams since he first began to scratch notes to himself on scraps of papyrus. Horses terrified our ancestors and they are still capable of frightening and killing us today.

Additionally, I realize in advance that an entrenched portion of the modern equestrian world will have strong reason to denounce this analysis of historical events. There are tremendous financial stakes involved in admitting that horses are not timid grass-eaters who are afraid of predatory mankind.

I am reminded though of what the military historian, Graham Clark, wrote regarding the theme of cultural antagonism.

"The importance of the horse in human history is matched only by the difficulties inherent in its study; there is hardly an incident in the story which is not the subject of controversy, often of a violent nature."

Likewise, there may be academic critics who assert that the equestrian world has no place for independent investigators such as myself.

Luckily, His Royal Highness, the Duke of Edinburgh, has long championed an alliance between lucid scientists and enthusiastic amateurs. He said, "Many of our pioneering engineers started without any formal training but had a passion, and a talent, for invention and development. The system does not seem to be able to cope with the 'hands-on' enthusiast, who has no immediate interest in academic qualifications."

Nor is the horse world bereft of such mounted examples. Carl Linnaeus, the father of biology, and Charles Darwin, the evolutionist, were both enthusiastic Historical Long Riders, whose contributions to science are still remembered. Likewise, another amateur, Mary Littauer, is credited with documenting the history of the chariot. Thus, throughout history an occasional lone wolf has defied the pundits and proved learned opinion wrong.

I don't pretend to have all the answers regarding deadly horses. All I have done is open a previously undetected door. What you find within is up to you.

Enduring Secrets

It is the most beloved and enduring equestrian legend of all time, the gentle equine friend, the trusted four-footed pal, the wise rescuer, the angelic messenger. Regardless if you call them Black Beauty, Trigger or "my friend Flicka," all the names are linked to a warm and comfortable story which states that the horse is a gentle herbivore from which we have nothing to fear.

What if that wasn't accurate?

What if conflicting evidence reveals that throughout history horses have been potentially lethal animals who kill lions, hyenas, pumas, wolves, tigers – and humans?

The modern world has been led to believe a recently-created animal myth which says horses are benign angels who fear man.

What if it could be proved instead that throughout history horses have had the biological capability, and desire, to consume a wide variety of meat – including humans?

An international multi-million dollar industry serviced by horse whisperers, glossy magazines and popular culture preaches that horses are meek prey animals.

What if evidence demonstrated horses can be eager hunters, predators and warriors, just like their riders?

Contemporary writers have successfully airbrushed murderous and meat-eating horses out of literature.

What if Shakespeare, Sherlock Holmes and Steve McQueen provided artistic evidence to refute that claim?

Thanks to wide-spread equestrian amnesia, the vital role played by horses in recent history has been lost to mankind.

What if crucial eyewitness testimony revealed that meat-eating horses had been used to explore the North and South Poles?

What if meat-eating horses had been found on every continent? What if six thousand years of equestrian wisdom had been misinterpreted or buried? What if the horses whom mankind dotes on and trusts were hiding a series of dark and blood-soaked secrets?

If that is indeed the case, then it might be said that the greatest equine deception of all times has been perpetrated by - the horses!

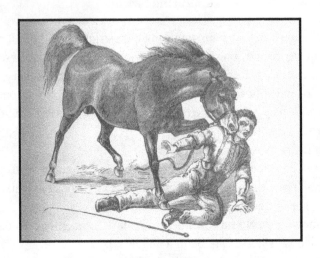

Though the majority of the modern world believes horses are benign grass eaters, research has confirmed that they are capable of attacking and consuming a wide variety of other animals, including man.

Likewise, contemporary mythology states that horses are hapless prey animals who flee from predators, when in reality ample evidence proves that horses can kill lions, pumas, hyenas and humans.

A Plea for Help

These seemingly impossible questions arose in 2002 when the Long Riders' Guild Academic Foundation became aware of a disturbing report which originated in the United States. According to that country's leading equine veterinarian publication, *The Horse*, readers had recently reported cases of horses killing smaller animals and in some cases devouring their prey.

Gruesome details emerged when one horrified reader wrote to the magazine editor. The reader described how he and a friend had witnessed what they called a "bizarre and frightening" episode wherein a horse grabbed a goat, shook it to death, and began devouring it. To add to their revulsion, a few minutes later the two startled witnesses observed three other horses approach the dead goat. They too begin consuming the flesh and drinking its blood.

"They all grabbed some part of the goat with their teeth and literally tore it into pieces with all the tugging and pulling. The one who had killed the goat had the biggest part of what was left.... Soon, two little colts less than three months old came over to what was left of the goat and they took some bites and just stood there chewing and eating.... My friend and I were absolutely stunned over what we had just witnessed."

In one of the three original letters addressed to the editors of *The Horse* magazine, this same bewildered eyewitness posed a question.

"The events we saw are still a mystery. Neither of us is willing to believe that this is the first time in history that something like this has ever happened with horses. There must be other people who have seen, read stories about, or know of similar events, and I am personally interested in knowing if anyone associated with your magazine has ever had any knowledge of anything like this happening in the past. We would feel better if we knew other people had witnessed something like this."

The horse owners were understandably upset and the editors eventually announced that they had no clue as to what might have motivated this bizarre equine behaviour.

(*Carnivorous Horses* by Dr. Sue McDonnell, *The Horse* – October, 2002, page 61.)

A Search for the Truth

That original disclosure led to an extraordinary international research project carried out by The Long Riders' Guild Academic Foundation. Equestrian explorers and researchers from a variety of countries pooled their experiences, delved into obscure documents, reviewed rare books and conducted interviews around the world so as to assist the author to investigate what most horse riders would consider to be a contradiction in terms – carnivorous and murderous horses.

After nine years of ground-breaking analysis, The Long Riders' Guild Academic Foundation compiled a list of incidents involving deadly horses and meat-eating equines which occurred around the world. Located in thirty countries over a space of nearly four thousand years, these horses consumed eighteen different types of flesh, including human beings.

Antelope	Horse	Seal
Beef	Human	Sheep
Birds	Moose	Tiger
Chicken	Offal	Whale
Fish	Onager	Yak
Goat	Polar Bear	
Hamster	Rabbits	

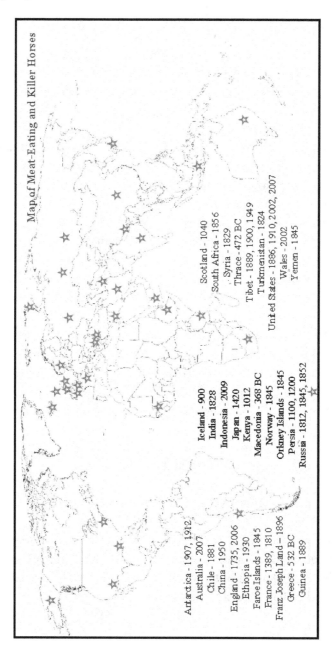

A list of incidents involving deadly horses and meat-eating equines which occurred on every continent.

The O'Reilly Anomaly

In addition to the discovery that equines were capable of consuming flesh, the LRG-AF study also disclosed that throughout recorded history humanity had routinely endured astonishing cases of homicidal horses.

How could this be?

According to modern popular culture the horse is a flight animal, a prey species, a gentle herbivore. Meat-eating and man-killing horses are thus believed to be biologically impossible. Yet what if the equine was found to be an omnivorous predator?

To understand that possibility, we must realize that an anomaly is a deviation from what is regarded as normal, something that is strange or unusual, any event that is out of the ordinary - but not impossible!

The O'Reilly Anomaly is the first study of the historical evidence documenting the existence of this type of equine aggression and dietary deviation.

Readers, however, must be warned. What has been discovered is at times so disturbing that life-long horsemen and hardened equestrian explorers have been severely shocked. It is not the goal of this study to distress the reader, only to educate the public about the past and warn horse owners that the same behaviour is bound to reappear in the future.

In order to accomplish these goals, we must realize that the first clues to deadly horses are found at the dawn of time.

Modern Problem, Ancient Answer

Why were the classical Greeks so terrified of the mounted people lurking outside their nation's borders? Could this Anomaly have been an undisclosed element of their original terror? Did the Greeks fear that they would be fed to the attacker's horses?

Those questions tie in to the original article published in 2002. When the readers of the veterinarian magazine sought clarification regarding the existence of meat-eating horses, the American magazine editors should have looked to ancient Greece for answers. These editors had forgotten the accursed mares of Diomedes. That gruesome tale recounts the first famous case of anthropophagic (man-eating) horses.

Mythical Roots

According to ancient Greek legend, King Diomedes of Thrace owned four mares named Podargos, Lampon, Xanthos and Deinos. These savage equines were fed on the human flesh of any hapless stranger unlucky enough to visit the despot's kingdom on the shores of the Black Sea.

The Grecian playwright, Euripedes, and the historian, Apollodorus, both recounted how Hercules was given the task of capturing these murderous horses and bringing them back to Greece. Several Grecian champions were invited to accompany Hercules on the voyage to Thrace. Upon their arrival, while Hercules fought the army of King Diomedes, his companion, Abderos, was tasked with guarding the murderous mares. While Hercules was occupied in battle, Abderos was killed and consumed by the meat-loving mares.

Ironically, in an act of ultimate equestrian revenge, when Hercules overthrew the dictator, the legendary strongman "cast the tyrant's still quivering carcass to his own horses to be devoured." In one version of the myth, the act of consuming the king made the mares docile. Hercules took the horses back to Greece, where they were set free. (*http://users.forthnet.gr/kat/antikas/Chapter28.htm*
The Horse in History by Basil Tozer, Methuen & Co., London, 1908.)

Even though Hercules supposedly defeated the man-eating horses of Diomedes in 472 B.C., the danger of this type of horses was still common knowledge in the sixteenth century and was referred to in *The Faerie Queene,* the English epic poem by Edmund Spenser, published in 1590.

What has been largely lost to modern mankind's collective consciousness is how these murderous mares may have influenced the military career of Alexander the Great.

This painting by Gustave Moreau depicts King Diomedes being devoured by his man-eating mares.

The Untold Story of Bucephalus

From the Gates of Hercules to the plains of Persia, there is a collection of tales describing how Alexander earned his nickname, "the Great." He sliced through the insolvable Gordian Knot. He vanquished the ancient world. He conquered the fearsome stallion, Bucephalus.

Born in 356 BC, Alexander went on to control the vast majority of the classic world, thereby putting countless people to the sword. Nevertheless his reputation has never suffered calamity like his fellow fearsome victor, Genghis Khan. The reasons for this are varied, yet one element of the Macedonian's personal myth which continues to endear Alexander to the public is the story of how the adolescent prince began his march to power by taming the wild Bucephalus.

Alongside the Victorian era's interest in Tiny Tim and Santa Claus, a benign equestrian fable also took root in children's nursery books. It recounted how brave little Alexander turned mighty Bucephalus away from his frightening shadow.

According to that version of events, which is now deeply embedded in the mind of modern man, when only thirteen years of age Alexander was present when a horse dealer delivered a beautiful steed to the boy's father, King Philip. The animal had been named Bucephalus, ox-head, because of the white spot on his nose shaped like an ox.

King Philip of Macedonia, a keen cavalryman who ruled a burgeoning military kingdom, greatly admired the horse. Unfortunately, a series of grooms was unable to ride Bucephalus, as one after the other, these experienced horsemen were tossed to the ground by the fiery stallion.

Eventually the disgruntled monarch ordered the horse to be removed, expressing his belief that a man would be a fool to purchase such an ill-tempered brute. At that moment the young prince stepped forward and begged permission to try and ride the apparently untameable horse.

This request induced the king to express his scorn. How, he asked, could a mere boy ride a horse which the professional grooms had been unable to handle? Ignoring his father's criticism, Alexander persisted with his claim, until the king relented.

Though he had his doubts that Alexander could even mount Bucephalus, Philip told his son that if he could ride the unruly stallion, the intrepid boy could keep him as his own mount.

While sources vary, the result of Alexander's request to ride Bucephalus contains the elements of the same story.

"The young prince then quietly walked up to the excited horse, took the bridle, held it firmly, and began to speak gently and pat the steed's arched neck. After a moment, Alexander led Bucephalus forward a few steps, and then turned him around, for he had noticed that the horse was frightened by his shadow.

Then, when the shadow lay where he could not see it, and where it could no longer frighten him, the young man dropped his cloak quietly, and vaulted upon the horse's back. Once more Bucephalus reared, pranced, kicked, and ran; but Alexander sat firmly on his back, spoke to him gently, and, making no effort to hold him in, let him speed across the plain. In a few moments the horse's wildness was over, and Alexander could ride back to his proud father, sitting upon a steed which obeyed his slightest touch."

(http://www.mainlesson.com/display.php?author=guerber&book=gree ks&story=steed)

According to this version of events, by simply turning the horse towards the sun, the clever Alexander won the horse which then carried him thousands of miles, from Macedonia to India, where the mighty horse finally died from battle wounds at the advanced age of thirty. According to the commonly-told tale, the grief-stricken Alexander honoured his beloved war horse by renaming the city he had conquered Bucephala.

The darker story of how Alexander tamed the man-eating Bucephalus has been white-washed out of history in favour of a children's fairy tale

But being clever wasn't enough to keep you on the throne in those blood-soaked days. That is why throughout his own brief life Alexander provided repeated evidence designed to demonstrate that he was more than human, that his courage was above that of ordinary men. According to one legend, the infant Alexander strangled a viper which had crept into his cradle. Stories such as these were designed to demonstrate his strength. Likewise, a now-neglected story involving Bucephalus provided additional startling evidence to Macedonian sceptics, not of how clever the young prince was, but proof of the fact that he possessed the raw courage needed to assume command of his father's military kingdom.

In the biography of Alexander written by the ancient Greek author, Plutarch, there are anecdotes and descriptions of events which appear in no other source. One legend recounts how the meat-eating mares of King Diomedes begat offspring who travelled north to Macedonia and thereafter served as the cavalry mounts of King Phillip. Alexander the Great's legendary steed, Bucephalus, was said to be descended from King Diomedes' killer equines.

Because he was descened from these murderous mothers, according to Plutarch's biography, a drastically different version of events lay behind Alexander's conquest of Bucephalus. The horse was not simply unmanageable. He was anthropophagous, a man-eating combatant that tore his foes and devoured their flesh.

In this unfamiliar version of the story, Bucephalus was presented to King Philip as a courtly gift. When the monarch realized the stallion devoured its enemies, Philip ordered the stallion to be confined in an iron cage. Thereafter disobedient subjects were thrown in and consumed by the carnivorous equine.

In Plutarch's story, when the fifteen-year-old Alexander visited the captive Bucephalus he observed two things; the animal's striking appearance and the remains of the numerous men he had slaughtered. Yet, despite being fully aware of the mortal danger he faced upon approaching Bucephalus, in an act of cold kingly courage, Alexander ordered the cage door to be unlocked. Once the reluctant guards obeyed, the young prince entered the cage, grabbed Bucephalus' mane and leapt on to his back. Alexander then rode the terrifying horse through the streets of Pella, his father's capital, thereby impressing his future subjects with further proof of his divinity, courage and horsemanship.

Mounted on the carnivorous Bucephalus, Alexander soon set off on his first military campaign, the result being that King Nicholas of Peloponnesus was defeated by the budding Macedonian sovereign. Not only had Alexander defeated his father's enemies, he had demonstrated his right to rule by taming a murderous equine.
(*http://1stmuse.com/alex3/bucephalus2.html*)

Dangerous warriors mounted on flesh-eating horses? Surely such a thing was nothing more than the invention of a fertile Greek imagination?

The Dappled Demon of Japan

But 1,750 years later and 8,000 miles away, horse history repeated itself.

From Pella, Macedonia, the Long Riders' Guild research led to Sagami, Japan, where another remarkable national myth was discovered lurking in the shadows. Like its predecessor, this tale also concerned a young prince mounted on a man-eating horse.

The legend of the wandering samurai, Oguri Hangan, is an old saga from Japan's pantheon of literary classics. It describes the travels and adventures of young Oguri, who lived from 1398 to 1464. During that time he made history by surviving and riding the Dappled Demon of Japan. Unlike Alexander, Oguri's encounter with a homicidal horse came about because of love.

Having learned from a roving peddler of a beautiful princess named Terute, Oguri determined to win her heart. He began this romantic siege by having the peddler deliver his love letters to Terute. Once the Japanese Juliet assured her lover that his passion was reciprocated, the headstrong Oguri rushed into her father's castle and demanded Terute's hand in marriage.

Though Lord Yokoyama pretended to accept his daughter's suitor, the outraged father decided to have Oguri slain thanks to a cunning trick. He wouldn't lay a hand on the upstart bridegroom himself. Quite the contrary. Yokoyama planned instead to let the man-eating Dappled Demon kill and consume the hated opponent.

Thus, in accordance with custom, Yokoyama hosted a tremendous banquet in honour of his daughter's marriage to Oguri. At the conclusion of that sumptuous meal, the treacherous Yokoyama called upon his son-in-law to entertain the aristocrats and samurai assembled there.

The unsuspecting bridegroom announced, "My talents include archery, or the knife, feats of strength or speed. Quick, tell me what you would enjoy."

"No," replied Yokoyama, "I have another challenge in mind."

The wily father-in-law then baited his hook by describing a horse he had recently purchased. Having down-played the animal as being just a back-country brute in need of a talented rider, Yokoyama dared Oguri to accept the ordeal. Little did Yokoyama know that among his many talents, Oguri was the most extraordinary horsemen in the history of the island kingdom.

"Even though he's wild, I'm sure you're man enough to ride him," Yokohama said, all the while hiding his true menace.

When the hero agreed, Yokoyama led his son-in-law and guests outside the castle and into the nearby countryside. There awaiting Oguri was the man-eating terror known as the Dappled Demon.

With the wedding guests following close behind, Yokoyama brought Oguri to the edge of the most fearsome enclosure ever described in equestrian history.

The first line of defence was a large moat. On the other side of this watery barrier was a corral designed to hold a fiend.

Eight pillars, standing to the right and left, had been firmly jammed into the ground. They were made of camphor tree trunks so huge it had required eighty-five men to transport each one from the mountains. Between these eight giants Oguri saw smaller pillars had been firmly driven into the ground. These pillars were made from strong chestnut trees and each of them was the span of three men's arms. As a final precaution, iron grating had been put into place between all the pillars, so as to complete the confinement.

While the mighty prison was a dire omen, what lay inside its walls left no doubt as to the murderous occupation of its sole inhabitant. Oguri instantly saw that the ground was littered with human skeletons. The crushed bones of these previous victims were in ample evidence. Scraps of their hair rustled among the human debris.

Inside this mighty fortress of death, surrounded by trophies of his previous kills, stood a single animal. Confronting Oguri was the terrifying, man-eating horse called Onikage, the Dappled Demon. Each of the Demon's grey fetlocks was festooned with a massive chain which attached him in four directions to the enormous camphor pillars. One look at the remains of the Demon's manly meals was all it took for Oguri to realize that it was his human intelligence, not his strength, which was needed.

Even though he realized the extent of his future father-in-law's treachery, Oguri crossed the moat, entered the fortress and walked straight up to the glowering stallion. To the astonishment of the on-lookers, the Japanese horseman then began to subdue the killer, not by brutality, but by reason.

"Greetings, Onikage," Oguri said quietly. "If you are a sentient being, prick up your ears and listen to me carefully. Other horses are kept tethered in ordinary stables. You are locked away in a grim prison. Other horses eat the green fodder brought to them by caring grooms. You instead devour those who attempt to help you. Other horses obey their masters. You kill anyone who tries to ride you.

In exchange for their valuable service, other horses are treated with kindness. Because they allow men to ride them, these horses are often tethered outside the temple gate. While their master attends the cere-mony inside, these horses can hear the prayers and those sutra readings remind the horses to consider their own future incarnations."

Though the crowd standing beyond the moat could not hear Oguri, it was clear even from a distance that the young horseman's words were having an astonishing effect on the murderous horse.

"For reasons I don't understand, you enjoy eating humans, Onikage. Those acts have turned you into a devil. The lives of people are sacred, as is yours. When you kill and eat a person, what do you suppose that does to you, Dappled Demon?"

Instead of slaying the impudent man, the man-killer stood listening intently.

"I don't care about your past sins, Onikage. In fact I have come to seek your assistance. If you will allow me to ride you, in order to honour your spirit, upon your death I vow to build a golden temple and place a statue of your likeness inside. All I ask in return is for your obe-dience and loyalty," Oguri said.

It was at that moment that Lord Yokoyama's plan went badly awry, because in front of the assembled samurai lords, Onikage the man-

slayer folded his front legs in reverence to Oguri. To their astonishment, the banquet guests saw golden tears of gratitude flowing from the
eyes of the great horse. As if in confirmation of his repentance, the
Dappled Demon then rose and stood completely still while Oguri undid
the mighty chains securing the stallion's legs.

Feeling himself free, Onikage shook his body violently and
screamed with pleasure. His trumpeting frightened Yokoyama and his
guests, but while they hesitated, trying to decide if they should stay or
flee, Oguri grabbed a handful of the Demon's mane and leapt upon his
bare back.

In a story which mirrors Alexander's, Oguri also conquered a man-
killing stallion and went on to win glory.

Before they could be stopped, Oguri rode the Dappled Demon
through the gates of his prison, jumped the moat, scattered the startled
guests and charged straight towards Lord Yokoyama's castle. With the
samurai running behind him, Oguri then proceeded to use his secret
knowledge of horses to accomplish a series of tasks which has never
been repeated nor reported outside Japan. According to the chronicles
Oguri rode Onikage up a ladder, across the castle roof and down a pine
tree. Upon emerging in front of the banquet hall, where stood the
assembled guests, Oguri urged the horse to jump up on a small go
(chess) board, where the Dappled Demon balanced upon his hind legs.

At the conclusion of these amazing feats, the clamour of admiration from the guests was so great that Lord Yokoyama felt compelled to present Oguri with ten horses laden with gold and treasure.

Though he encountered many other terrible adventures, Oguri and Terute were eventually able to live together in his castle. Thanks to his courage, by the 15th century the valiant samurai was worshipped in Japan as that country's god of war.

He never forgot his promise to the reformed Dappled Demon. Using Lord Yokoyama's gold, Oguri built the promised temple and erected a statue of the fearsome horse, who remains venerated as an equine deity in Japan.

(*www.persee.fr/web/revues/home/prescript/article/asie_0766-1177_2002_num_13_1_1187   Page 369*)

A grisly alternative tale about Bucephalus? A man-eating horse still being worshipped in Japan? Are there hitherto unexplored equestrian legends linking the Orient and Europe?

When you consider the similarities between Bucephalus and Oni-kage, one wonders why these versions of events have remained largely invisible for so many centuries?

Could it be linked to an undiagnosed global case of wilful equine blindness?

Wilful Blindness

In the ancient world, Cassandra's woeful predictions were routinely ignored. Today scientists have developed a term to describe how humans filter out information that contradicts their world view or threatens their beliefs. They call it wilful blindness or confirmation bias.

Though the prophetess was only pointing out the obvious, her fellow Trojans preferred to disregard the frightening and painful reality she was revealing. Instead of embracing the difficult truth, they believed their strong sense of denial would protect them. This collective delusion left them vulnerable to peril.

Like Trojan soldiers, the majority of modern mankind is taught from infancy to conform to social authority, to agree with the echo chamber of popular opinion, to belong rather than to question. It feels seductive to be safe. It is distressing to contradict one's previous equestrian beliefs. Most of us are bound to the wheel of intellectual convention.

It does no good to turn a blind eye towards the existence of murderous horses, for the warning signs of its continued existence are in plain sight, if one but looks.

To predict the future, one must look to the past.

The Truth behind the Myth

Of course the tales of Bucephalus and Onikage were only gory myths, tales of "night mares" which were better ignored in this age of pampered paddock potatoes. Who could put any stock into such a fierce fairytale?

But are all myths merely fantasy? Is there a kernel of truth buried within? The answer lies in science, not mythology.

For example, in 2010 a zoologist at Great Britain's Cambridge university observed that a rook could solve an ancient and complicated riddle. When presented with a pitcher partly filled with water, the clever bird deduced that by dropping stones into the pitcher, it could raise the level of the precious fluid. Moreover, the rook realised that by dropping the largest stones in first, he would raise the water level more quickly.

(*Inside the Minds of Animals* by Jeffrey Kluger, Time magazine, August 16, 2010, page 24)

Why does this matter? Because in 500 BC the Greek author, Æsop, had written a tale about a bird who had been able to achieve this difficult task. Yet it had taken 2500 years for a scientist to prove the story was not a myth.

Nor was this the first time curious modern humans had uncovered similar discoveries.

In 1870 the German archaeologist Heinrich Schliemann excavated a hill in modern-day Turkey and discovered the "lost" city of Troy awaiting him. More recently, the Italian archaeologist Andra Carandini discovered evidence indicating that Romulus and Remus, the legendary founders of Rome, had actually existed.

So if Achilles and Romulus had once walked the Earth, then why not King Diomedes and his meat-eating mares?

When the LRG-AF began its preliminary investigation, we too discovered a startling equestrian fact buried in Greek history. When the sixty-third Olympics were held in 532 B.C., Cimon of Athens arrived nursing a grudge. During the previous Olympic games four years earlier, the noted chariot racer had lost to his arch rival, Pisistratus. Consequently when the time came for the two rivals to race again, Cimon prepared for the competition by feeding his chariot team a meat diet rather than the dried figs they usually ate.

Nor were the clues restricted merely to ancient historical sources.

When the LRG-AF began using its international network of equestrian contacts to query the bizarre equine predators observed by readers of the American magazine, we were stunned at the evidence awaiting our scrutiny.

African Horse Horror

It was in France that we uncovered many early clues.

To begin with, French law journals had recorded that in 1389 a horse in Dijon was condemned to death for having killed a man.

Then French Long Rider Jean-Louis Gouraud, whose grandfather had served as a colonial officer in Africa, provided the Guild with our first eyewitness account of meat-eating horses.

Gouraud's grandfather had reported that in December, 1889 his horse had killed and eaten a chicken in front of the entire village. "I am still riding my little horse Kourma, who is indefatigable. One day, I set myself up for the day under a lovely tree, the village being very crowded, with hot and narrow streets. Youssouffi, my little groom, who had taken my horse to the village, came running back. 'Come quickly! Come quickly! Kourma – he's eaten a hen! I always told you that he was a man!' I went there and found the entire village gathered together around the horse, who was quietly eating the millet spread for him on the ground. A chicken, quite large they told me, had come to peck at some and Kourma had eaten it in one mouthful."
(*L'Afrique, par Monts et par Chevaux* by Jean Louis Gouraud, Belin, Paris, 2003.)

A famed French Long Rider, author, publisher and film-maker, Gouraud also provided The Guild with this startling extract from a rare 1930s French account.

In his book, *The Ethiopian Drama,* Henry de Monfried related a horrific slaughter which incorporated meat-eating equines in African warfare. Monfried wrote, "The Assaïmaras decided one day to attack the Danakils. Two thousand men and six hundred horses set off along the sinuous track. The thin horses passed like shadows in the moonlight, as silent as shadows on this soft ground where their hooves make no noise. Their extreme thinness was not a weakness, for they are as indefatigable as the nomads of the desert who ride them. As is the warrior custom, these horses have been fed meat for months. They are trained to swallow goats' and sheep's entrails, still throbbing with life.

African warriors fed their war horses raw human flesh.

For three hours these shadows travel silently on the spongy ground; then they all disappear and solitude falls again on the immensity and the night resumes its calm. Suddenly, in the Danakil camp, where everyone was resting, a dog barks; the others, woken, join the chorus and howl like jackals. Then, at these cries of alarm, as if they were a signal, a rumbling – and the clamour of war!

Horses at full gallop surge forward, their riders bristling with lances. Taken by surprise while half asleep at dawn, the Danakils are shocked. With no time to defend themselves, the men quickly have their throats cut, are disembowelled and then mutilated. When the women are reached, they turned to face their adversaries in a vain attempt to protect their children. But the soldiers, their bodies glistening with butter and sweat, seize the children, who cry and struggle. Then, with one blow of his dagger, the warrior rips out the babe's heart and liver and throws them to his ravenous horse."

Nor were such shocking historical accounts confined to Africa! There was a host of overlooked clues waiting to be re-examined. For example, Marco Polo reported that the horsemen of southern Persia fed their horses dried fish.
(*www.fullbooks.com/The-Travels-of-Marco-Polo-Volume-220.html*)

Vikings and Bandits

More startling still was the Viking account from 900 A.D. regarding another man-eating equine. Entitled *Snaekoll's Saga*, the legendary tale was saved for posterity by the Long Rider author, Don Roberto Cunninghame Graham. According to this Icelandic legend, Thor Grimur Hjaltalin was a famous warrior and traveller who owned a notoriously vicious stallion named Snaekoll, "who had a bite worse than a walrus." This savage iron-grey was unrideable by anyone but his owner, who fed him on "salt cod or on dried whale beef, and for that reason was not quite safe to leave alone with sheep when they had lambs. But for all that, Thor Grimur did not care, and never grudged a lamb or two when he reflected that his horse could go fifty miles a day for a whole week and be just as fresh at the end as when he left."

Though others had crossed difficult parts of Iceland, no one had yet ridden across the two-hundred mile long frozen wasteland known as the Vatna Jokull. So in spring, Thor ignored local advice, saddled the grey stallion and pointed him towards the great icy desert which was said to be haunted by evil spirits.

Mounted on Snaekoll, the Icelandic traveller rode into the wilderness and was never seen again. The horse eventually emerged on the other side of the wilderness, having survived, according to legend, by eating his rider.

(*Tales of Horsemen* by R.B. Cunninghame Graham, The Long Riders' Guild Press, Zürich, 2004.)

While the calendar marched on from the tenth century, tales of meat-eating and murderous horses continued to flourish.

In 1851, John Cremony survived what became known as the "Journey of Death." During a solo trip across New Mexico, Cremony was attacked by Apaches. The resultant chase saw Cremony ride 125 miles in 24 hours, the last 70 miles at the gallop. Having outraced his murderous pursuers, on arrival at the village of Dona Ana, the weary horseman rubbed his horse with soft straw until he was dry, a process that took two hours. Next he washed the horse with a mixture of whisky and water, then again rubbed him dry. Then the horse's shoes were removed. After wrapping the horse in blankets, Cremony sprinkled hay with water and mixed in raw, chopped steak. The exhausted rider then dropped into his own bed.

(*A Ride through the Journey of Death* by Cindy Hayostek, *Horse & Rider* magazine, January, 1988, page 50.)

Cremony's decision to feed his horse raw steak may have been based upon an inherited equestrian tradition brought to the New World from England.

According to legend, the famous English highwayman, Dick Turpin, was able to elude capture in 1735 by tying a beef-steak round the bit of his famous mare, Black Bess. This enabled her to race from London to York and escape the law, "after being animated by the juice of the beef-steak."

(*The Horse and his Rider* by Rollo Springfield, Chapman & Hall, London, 1847)

Outlaw Dick Turpin eluded the authorities thanks to the extraordinary strength his mare, Black Bess, derived from her meat-eating diet.

The Deadliest Horse

While that tale might be apocryphal, what is certain is that the celebrated French cavalry officer, Baron de Marbot, left an astonishing narrative of the man-killing horse he rode during the Napoleonic invasion of Russia in 1812. This mare, Lisette, became infamous in France when she disembowelled her groom.

"Having two good horses for the coming campaign, I was looking for a third even better specimen to be my charger. It was a difficult thing to find, for though horses were far less dear than now, I had very little money; but chance served me admirably. I met a learned German, Herr von Aister, whom I had known when he was a professor at Soreze. He had become tutor to the children of a rich banker, Monsieur Scherer, established at Paris in partnership with Monsieur Finguerlin. He informed me that Monsieur Finguerlin – a wealthy man living in fine style – had a large stud, in the first rank of which figured a lovely mare called Lisette. She was reputedly easy in her paces, as light as a deer, and so well broken that a child could lead her. But this mare, in fact, had a terrible fault: she bit like a bulldog and furiously attacked people whom she disliked; and this had determined Monsieur

Finguerlin to sell her. She was bought for Madame de Lauriston, whose husband (one of the Emperor Napoleon's aides de camp), had written to her to get his campaigning outfit ready. When selling the mare, Monsieur Finguerlin had forgotten to mention her fault and that every evening a groom was found disembowelled at her feet."

The lady was "reasonably alarmed" and the police ordered that "a written statement should be placed in Lisette's stall to inform prospective purchasers of her ferocity." Because of the animal's murderous nature the Baron was able to purchase her for a fraction of what she was worth. The animal gave Marbot a good deal of trouble for months. It took four or five men to saddle her and she could only be bridled by covering her eyes and binding all four legs. Once seated upon her back, she was an incomparable mount. The problem lay in learning how to handle this dangerous horse.

"Lisette proved to be a demon. She had already bitten several people while in my possession (not even sparing me) and I was thinking that perhaps I should part with her, when I engaged in my service one Francis Woirland, a man who was afraid of nothing. He had heard of Lisette's bad character and before approaching her, armed himself with a hot roast leg of mutton. When the animal flew at him he held out the mutton – which she seized in her teeth – and burning her gums, palate and tongue, gave out a scream of agony, letting the mutton drop. From that moment Lisette was perfectly submissive to Woirland and did not venture to attack him again. I employed the same method with a like result…"

Despite her savage nature, Baron de Marbot was mounted on the murderous mare at the battle of Eylau, which occurred in Prussia in February, 1807. At the height of the fighting, the Emperor Napoleon decided to order one of his regiments to retreat. It was, however, a suicidal task for any Napoleonic officer to ride through the mass of Russian troops which surrounded the besieged soldiers. Regardless of the danger, the dashing Marbot volunteered. Having survived a swarm of Cossacks and a hail of bullets, Marbot and Lisette reached the relative safety of the French line. They had no sooner arrived when the Russians mounted another furious attack.

During the Napoleonic wars, the French hussar officer, Baron Marbot, rode his mare Lisette into battle. In one horrific battle, Lisette killed and ate a Russian soldier.

"Bullets whistled past my ear and one of them would certainly have taken away the small amount of life left in me had not a terrible incident led to my escape from this murderous mêlée.

Among the Frenchmen pressing against my mare's flanks was a quartermaster-sergeant whom I recognised. This man, having been attacked and wounded by several of the enemy, fell under Lisette's belly and was seizing my leg to pull himself up, when a Russian grenadier, too drunk to stand steady, attempted to finish him with a thrust to the breast. The Russian, losing his balance, plunged his bayonet into my cloak, which at that moment was puffed out by the wind. Seeing that I did not fall, the grenadier left the sergeant and aimed a great number of blows at me, eventually piercing my left arm. I felt with a kind of horrible pleasure my blood flowing warmly. The Russian, with redoubled fury, made another thrust at me but, stumbling with the force which he had put into it, drove his bayonet straight into Lisette's thigh.

Her ferocity restored by the pain, she sprang at the Russian and at one mouthful tore off his nose and all the skin of his face, making of him a living death's head, dripping with blood. Then, hurling herself with fury among the combatants, kicking and biting, Lisette upset everything in her path. When a Russian officer tried to hold her by the bridle she seized him by his belly and carrying him off with ease, bore him out of the crush to the foot of the hillock where, having torn out his entrails and mashed his body under her feet, she left him dying in the snow."

Despite being wounded himself, the Baron wrote that "thanks to my Hussar's saddle I kept my seat," after which Lisette galloped him towards safety. There French doctors tended to the Baron's wounds by "rubbing my body with rum."   They made bandages for Lisette by "cutting up the shirt of a dead soldier", after which they both began their long march to recovery.

(*The Memoirs of Baron de Marbot, Late Lieutenant General in the French Army* by Joseph Marbot, Longmans, London, 1892)

Also of note was the fact that, prior to his discovery of the extensive ruins of ancient Petra, the famous Swiss explorer, Johann Burckhardt, wrote in 1829 that the horses in Syria were fed roasted meat before the commencement of a fatiguing journey.

(*The Horse and his Rider* by Rollo Springfield, Chapman & Hall, London, 1847)

Less than twenty years later, in 1845, the *Edinburgh Journal of Natural History* reported, "It is said to be a common practice in some parts of India to mix animal substances with the grain given to feeble horses, and to boil the mixture into a sort of paste, which soon brings them into good condition, and restores their vigour.... The Russian serf make use of the dried flesh of the hamster reduced to powder, and mixed with oats; and that this occasions their horses to acquire a sudden and extraordinary degree of good health. Anderson relates, in his *History of Iceland*, that the inhabitants feed their horses with dried fishes when the cold is very intense, and that these animals are

extremely vigorous, though small. We also know that in the Feroe [sic]
Islands, the Orkneys, the Western Islands, and in Norway, where the
climate is very cold, this practice is also adopted;   and it is not
uncommon in some very warm countries, – as in the kingdom of
Muskat, in Arabia Felix, near the straits of Ormuz, one of the most
fertile parts of Arabia, fish and other animal substances are there given
to the horses in the cold season, as well as in times of scarcity."

*There are various accounts of horses disembowelling humans and
consuming their flesh. This 16th century woodcut matches the actions of
the murderous French mare, Lisette, who killed and ate her Russian
victim.*

Terror in India

At the same time as meat-eaters were under discussion in Scotland,
the London horse world was rocked by the revelation that a former
royal equine had turned man-killer in India.

According to two different nineteenth century English authors,
Great Britain's King George IV presented a beautiful bay thoroughbred

to his fellow monarch, the Maharaja of Oude. An eye-witness, Colonel Davidson, reported seeing this stallion after it had been safely delivered to the Maharaja's stable at Lucknow.

What transpired between the animal's arrival and its next confirmed sighting is unknown. Yet a short while later the noted journalist, William Knighton, left an amazing account of how the English horse had been transformed into a murderous equine monster which was terrorizing the city.

In his story, *The Man-Eater*, Knighton began by explaining how he barely escaped with his life when confronted by this destroyer.

"I was driving in a buggy one morning through one of the finest streets of Lucknow, proceeding with a friend to the Maharaja's palace. The deserted condition of the streets as we advanced surprised us. There was no inhabitant to be seen for a considerable distance."

At length, in the middle of the road, the two Englishmen came upon a trampled bloody mass which bore a resemblance to a human figure. When they stopped the buggy to satisfy their curiosity, they discovered it was the corpse of a native woman who had been terribly disfigured.

"The body was bruised and lacerated in all directions, the scanty drapery torn from the form; the face had been crushed as if by teeth into a shapeless mass; the long matted hair, which fell in bundles over the road, was all clotted with blood. It was altogether as disgusting a sight as one could well see anywhere. Apparently she was quite dead and we did not delay," Knighton wrote.

As the two companions continued their buggy ride, there was still no sign of life. All the houses were closed and a palpable sense of terror hung over the silenced city. A little further down the road, the English-men discovered a second victim, a youth who had been similarly mangled and destroyed. When they slowed their buggy to ascertain if that native was also dead, they noticed one of the king's troopers standing atop a nearby house. He was looking intently up the road along which the travellers were advancing.

Knighton called up to ask what was the matter?

"The man-eater is loose, sahibs," was the reply. Before the English-man could ask for a further explanation, the soldier shouted, "Look out! He has turned in our direction. Flee for your lives."

Thankfully, Knighton had heard of a savage horse that went by the name admee-kanawallah, the man-eater. But before the journalist could inform his companion, the soldier screamed, 'He is coming, sahibs. Take care, take care."

The sight which greeted the astonished Englishman defied description. A large bay stallion was trotting down the road towards them. Dangling from his mouth was a dead child, which the horse was shaking savagely.When he saw the men in the buggy, however, the horse threw the toddler on the road and immediately rushed to attack his new prey.

There wasn't a moment to lose.

"I rapidly turned the buggy round, though my horse was almost unmanageable with terror. Then we went flying back down the road at a mad gallop, heading towards an enclosure with iron gates we had passed a short time before. As we ran for our lives, we could hear the iron-shod hooves of the man-eater in hot pursuit."

The second they passed through the gates, Knighton's friend sprang from the buggy and slammed the gate shut.

"Just as the fall of the bolt secured our safety, the man-eater dashed up. His head was covered with blood, his jaws steaming with recent slaughter, his cheeks horrid with coagulated guts that had most probably spurted from his victims. There he stood, with cocked ears, distended nostrils and glaring eye-balls, looking savagely at us through the iron railings. My poor horse trembled as if shivering with cold at the sight of this ferocious-looking monster."

Having determined that he could not reach the Englishmen, the murderous horse returned to the road in search of other victims. His route took him under an archway built over the road. Here several troopers had prepared an ambush. A noose was thrown over the horse's head. He was then roped, thrown to the ground, and muzzled, before being conducted back to this stable.

With the equine assassin under control, Knighton concluded his journey to the Maharaja's palace. During their meal, he mentioned the circumstances of that day's eventful buggy ride.

'He is more savage than a tiger, your majesty.'

"A tiger – good – he shall fight a tiger. We shall see what impression my tiger, Burrhea, will make on him."

The following day Knighton, the Maharaja and his usual suite of attendants gathered in the gallery of a court-yard. It was sixty yards square, with buildings all round, and a veranda below. Thick bamboo railings had been placed in front of the veranda, so as completely to encircle the court-yard, and to form a sort of enlarged cage. The monarch and his guests commanded a full view of the court-yard.

The man-eater had been enticed into the enclosure by means of a small mare of trifling value. The order was then given and the tiger's cage was brought into the veranda. A door in the bamboo railings, prepared for the purpose, was drawn up. The cage door was opened and Burrhea bounded into the court-yard, lashing his long tail, and glaring furiously at the two horses.

Burrhea had been kept without food or drink from the previous day to prepare him for the assault. He glared savagely at the horses as he entered, and commenced slowly stealing along towards them. The man-eater kept his eyes fixed on his enemy. Not for an instant did he take them off; his head lowered, standing in an uneasy attitude with one foot slightly advanced, he awaited the attack, moving as the tiger moved, but always with the eyes intently fixed.

As for the poor little mare, she stood cowering in a corner, para-lysed with fear. Burrhea was upon her in an instant. A blow of his paw threw the mare to the ground, then he sank his teeth into her neck and drank her blood greedily.

'It will make Burrhea all the more savage,' predicted the Maharaja.

While the tiger enjoyed his draught of blood, the man-eater displayed no signs of uneasiness. Still standing at attention, he watched his enemy intently, as if prepared for immediate action. When the tiger had satisfied his thirst, he began to silently stalk the bay stallion. Knighton recalled that it was an unforgettable scene for the audience, who were straining their eyes and ears to catch every movement and every sound.

Then, without a warning of any kind, Burrhea sprang into the air, with claws and teeth aimed at his prey. The man-eater however was not taken by surprise. Once again he dodged the tiger's attack and once again his iron shod hooves smashed into the tiger. The blow threw the tiger to the ground.

Though the horse's haunches were bleeding, he resumed his former position and awaited his enemy. As the tiger paced round him, the man-eater watched as intently as ever. His head and neck were lowered, ears cocked, eyes fixed, one fore-foot slightly advanced in anticipation of the next attack.

After slaying a number of adults and children, the ferocious man-killer of Oude was forced by the Maharaja to fight a wild tiger. After being soundly beaten by the English Thoroughbred, the tiger was so terror-stricken, "his tail was between his legs and he ran round not unlike a whipped spaniel."

"When Burrhea regained his feet it was apparent he was desperate to escape, not attack again. His jaw was broken, and with his tail between his legs, he cried out piteously with pain as he ran round, not unlike a whipped spaniel."

The displeased ruler gave the signal that the tiger was to be removed. The door of the cage was opened and Burrhea rushed in to bury himself in the furthest corner. Though the man-eater had survived, his safety was short lived.

"Let another tiger be set at him," shouted the king to his servants. "Damn him. I will have my revenge for his destroying Burrhea."

That predator proved unwilling to attack the fierce stallion. He too was re-caged and removed. Finally the outraged ruler ordered the natives to drive three wild water buffalos into the courtyard. Surely now, the monarch predicted, the horse would be impaled on the horns of these angry beasts.

Not so.

"There is no animal so fierce and terrible as the wild buffalo," the Englishman reported, "as when aroused, wild water buffalo could even put elephants to flight."

When the buffalo came into the arena, the stallion retreated as they advanced into the middle of the court yard. Even the tigers had not disturbed him as did these monsters with their wide branching horns. The horse retreated step by step, snorting as he moved backwards. The buffalo huddled together, sniffing at the ground, glancing at the horse, and then staring at the maharaja as if to ask why they were there. The idea of attacking the man-eater never entered their heads.

The horse, however, took advantage of their uncertainty. He pawed the ground, then advanced step by careful step towards the clumsy brutes.

"Familiarity breeds contempt," wrote Knighton, and certainly it did so in this instance, for after advancing nearer, the man-eater suddenly wheeled round and began lashing out furiously against the ribs of the nearest buffalo."

The attack was so sudden and violent that the three buffalo were stunned, then moved away.

Having realized that the horse was once again undefeated, the maharaja laughed and announced, "By my father's head, the man-eater is a brave fellow who deserves to live."

The order was obeyed instantly. The horse was captured, muzzled and led to his stable, a victor and a conqueror.

True to his word, the Indian ruler ordered an iron cage made for the still dangerous horse. It was twice the size of many modern London dining-rooms. There, Knighton reports, the English stallion roamed inside the walls of his iron house, exhibiting his teeth to visitors and kicking the bars of his prison if strangers ventured too close.

"When I left Lucknow, the man-eater was still one of its sights," the journalist recalled.

(*The Man-Eater: An Ancient Story from the Private Life of an Eastern King* by William Knighton, republished by the Long Riders' Guild Academic Foundation, 2010. *www.lrgaf.org/articles/maneater.htm*)

Nor were these man-killers restricted to Asia, as another notorious equine outlaw was found terrorizing the United States at roughly the same time.

In a scene reminiscent of how the Man-Eater of Lucknow broke the tiger's jaw, recent evidence of equines defeating predators was discovered in the Ngorongoro Conservation area of Tanzania, where wildlife photographer, Thomas Whetten, witnessed this zebra successfully defending itself against a lion.

Death in the Americas

Professor Oscar R. Gleason, the best known equestrian trainer of his day, was at the height of his popularity when his "duel" with a man-killing equine occurred on April 19th, 1886 at the Cosmopolitan Hall in New York. There Gleason met the most savage horse of his career, the four-time man-killer known as Rysdyk.

"Rysdyk, the black-brown Hambletonian stallion who killed groom Brady by shaking him in his teeth, came to New York a week ago so wild that he had to be chained head and foot. His owner, J. H. Kimball, of Montreal, wanted to get rid of him at any cost, but could find no one to take him as a gift," reported the local newspaper. Gleason agreed to risk his life in an attempt to tame the murderous equine.

After being shackled and loaded on an express train, the Canadian horse was shipped from Montreal to New York.

By the following Monday local citizens were eagerly purchasing tickets, ready to see Gleason slain in public.

"The Cosmopolitan Theatre was crowded last night with people anxious to witness Prof. O. R. Gleason, the horse trainer, handle the vicious Canadian stallion that killed his groom a week ago. When people entered the house they saw a big brown horse standing inside an enclosure of board fence painted green. Professor Gleason appeared a few minutes after eight and spoke briefly to the audience. He intimated that most horses had more intelligence than their drivers, and after a few encouraging remarks entered the pen with the stallion, carrying a whip and a cocked revolver loaded with blank cartridges. He spoke to the animal in a loud tone, and then walked toward him. The stallion moved into a corner of the pen and turned his heels toward the professor.... Suddenly there was a cry from the audience. Like a flash the stallion had turned and seized the professor by the right forearm with his gleaming white teeth. The instructor dropped his whip, and with a violent effort wrenched his arm free. Then he fired the revolver several times in front of the brute's nose."

According to newspaper accounts of the day, Gleason tamed the man-killer in front of a standing-room-only crowd in less than an hour. (*The Science of Taming the Vicious* Horse by Prof. O.R. Gleason, Hubbard Publishing, Philadelphia, 1887)

While these examples were of tremendous historical interest, the Guild then uncovered information documenting how meat-eating horses were used to explore both the Arctic Circle and Antarctica.

Unlike European horses, which normally received more human interaction as they grew up, many 19th century North American horses retained a savage streak which resulted in numerous violent accidents and deaths to the horses' owners. Rysdyk was one such murderous equine.

North Pole Horses

While it is now commonly agreed that dog travel in winter conditions is an excellent methodology, abundant evidence demonstrates that this view was not shared by all polar explorers at the beginning of the last century. As the use of horses in the Arctic Circle and Antarctica prove, there was an on-going transportation debate at that time, not the open and shut case as is normally portrayed in the majority of today's books.

What has also been overlooked is the simultaneous use of meat-eating horses in trying to reach both the North and South Poles.

Likewise, it is wrong to think that the lack of any equine fodder in the Antarctic interior automatically ruled out horses, as once the explorer moves away from the seal and penguin populations there is also no meat for the dogs. Advocates of dog travel argue that as the expedition journeys further inland, dogs can be sacrificed and fed to their companions. Horses, it was believed, had to rely on grass or grain, brought at great effort from the coast.

During his crossing of Siberia, in the winter of 2004, Swedish Long Rider Mikael Strandberg, documented the still thriving Yakut equestrian culture. This local rider and his horse were photographed before setting off during minus sixty degree Celsius weather.

Recent discoveries demonstrate instead that a meat-eating horse would have reached the South Pole years before dogs did so, had he not fallen victim to an accident en route.

The decision to incorporate equine strength into Polar exploration was based upon the fact that the Siberian equestrian culture had a centuries-old tradition of winter-time horse travel. Despite having the coldest climate in the northern hemisphere, the Siberians routinely travelled along the great post road which criss-crossed that portion of the Russian empire. For example, Kolymsk merchants would carry cargo 2450 kilometres, from Yakutsk to Srednekolymsk, on the same horses. Their hardy Yakut horses not only endured minus sixty-degree winters, they were known to function well in deplorable and dangerous arctic conditions.

The horses are able to survive because they have specialized hair which has a core that greatly increases its insulating characteristics. Additional insulation is provided by a sub-dermal layer of fat. Plus, the Siberian horses have the ability to alter the rate of their respiration, thereby helping them to further adapt to extremes of cold weather. The Yakut horses were even known to function well while being covered in sheets of ice, which actually acted as an insulating agent.

(*The Yakuts – A Legendary Horse People* by Mikael Strandberg, published in 2005 by the Long Riders' Guild Press. *www.thelongridersguild.com/yakuts.htm*)

In 1893 a renowned British explorer and Long Rider, Frederick George Jackson, used these remarkable Russian horses to make a 3,000 mile winter crossing of Siberia. Thanks to the success of this expedition, in 1894 Jackson was asked to head an international expedition whose goal was to explore Franz Josef Land, a remote archipelago located north of Russia in the Arctic Ocean.

While Jackson did take dogs, he also brought four Siberian horses with him to explore this inaccessible part of the world, thus setting the stage for a significant set of equestrian events which would later conclude in Antarctica.

During Jackson's journey in Franz Josef Land with his robust horses, it was 30 degrees below zero (-34° C). Yet he travelled "night and day" for twelve days with a sledge weighing 700 pounds, covering 240 miles along "abominable tracks."

"And such are the courage and stamina of these hardy little Russian horses that although we had only given them two rests of two hours each during that time they were full of spirit at the end."

He later writes, "We had travelled 470 miles in seven and a half days; and I think this speaks volumes for the little Russian horses. We had two sledges, and one horse to each sledge; we went at a spanking pace nearly the whole way, yet they trotted into camp as fresh as paint."

The British explorer later wrote that he was, "thoroughly satisfied with my experiment … The horses had proved to be an unqualified success."

Upon his return from the Arctic Circle, the New York Times reported the avid horseman praised the animals as being "eat-all horses."

"The ponies proved by far the most useful animal for sledge dragging. They were hardy, and when the supply of oats and hay was exhausted, easily accustomed themselves to eating dry dog biscuit or bear meat."

In his book, Jackson recalled how one of these animals, a mare named Brownie, "appears to be doing very well on her miscellaneous diet. In addition to her regular feed of Spratt dog biscuits and hay, she shares the scraps left from our meals with the dogs, and very frequently helps herself to their polar bear meat, and shows a fondness for picking at bird skins lying around the hut."

(*A Thousand Days in the Arctic* by Frederick George Jackson, published by Harper & Brothers, New York, 1899.
In the Arctic North – Frederick Jackson's Account, New York Times Book Review –
http://query.nytimes.com/mem/archive-free/pdf?res=F70E16F73B5416738DDDAA0894DE405B8985F0D3)

Frederick George Jackson traversed Australia on a Brumby, sailed across the Atlantic on a whaler, made a legendary winter crossing of Siberia, then used meat-eating horses to explore the Arctic Circle. This illustration shows his favourite mare, Brownie, who ate polar bear meat.

Further horse journeys were to follow.

www.lrgaf.org

In 1901 and 1903 two American expeditions also explored the Arctic Circle, both of which used Siberian horses. The second attempt was led by a talented photographer, Anthony Fiala. The equestrian needs of that expedition were handled by veterans of the United States cavalry. These former Indian fighters "led the expedition in mounted drills and exercise rides on the Arctic ice."

Once again the horses proved to be of immense help.

"The ponies were less troublesome than the dogs and more powerful, dragging loads that astonished us all," Fiala reported. (*Fighting the Polar Ice* by Anthony Fiala, published by Hodder & Stoughton, London, 1907.)

In 1903 former United States cavalry soldiers were recruited to explore the Arctic Circle on horseback.

Shackleton and Socks

With these equestrian expeditions serving as a background, and thanks to positive personal experiences with his own meat-eating horses, Jackson encouraged Sir Ernest Shackleton also to use horses in the latter's bid to reach the South Pole. When the Irish explorer set out to explore Antarctica in 1907, he took ten Manchurian horses, thereby creating an exceptional chain of equestrian events which led from Siberia to the Arctic Circle, and then south to Antarctica.

Though it was later learned that horses will eat seal meat, Shackleton had no way of knowing this prior to his departure. In need of dietary advice, the sailor turned horse explorer turned to the military for assistance. What he found may surprise modern readers.

It has now been largely forgotten that when the British War Office published *Animal Management*, a manual prepared by the veterinarian department for His Majesty's Cavalry and Artillery, the index had a listing for "meat as horse food."

On page 103 it advised, "Meat was utilized successfully during the siege of Metz by being cut into small pieces and rolled in bran, and Norwegian stock of all kinds are accustomed to consume a soup made from boiled fish." Likewise, page 139 advises cavalry officers that riders in India and Turkmenistan were both "in the habit of giving their horses balls of meat."

(*Animal Management,* Prepared in the Veterinary Department for General Staff, War Office, London, HMSO, 1913.)

Even though these entries are not overly long, it confirms that the British military high command was aware that horses could consume meat-based rations under certain circumstances. The grassless ice fields of Antarctica would certainly have qualified.

To overcome the horse's need for bulk grass based feed, Shackleton arranged to purchase ten tons of compressed fodder consisting of oats, bran and chaff. He also took a large stock of corn. Yet upon the advice of the British military equestrian establishment, Shackleton decided to enhance his horses' normal diet with a special meat-based supplement known as "Maujee Ration." This was a distinctive type of equine pemmican developed at Aldershot, one of England's most important military establishments.

Sir Ernest recalled, "It consisted of dried beef, carrots, milk, currents and sugar, and was chosen because it provides a large amount of nourishment with comparatively little weight."

(*Heart of the Antarctic* by Sir Ernest Shackleton, published by William Heinemann, London, 1909.)

Shackleton set off for the Pole with three comrades and four of the original ten horses. Each of the Manchurian horses pulled a twelve-foot sledge carrying an average of 650 pounds. Like Jackson before him, Shackleton praised his horses.

"They are accustomed to hauling heavy loads in a very low temperature, and they are hardy, sure-footed and plucky."

*The majority of historians have overlooked, or misinterpreted, how
horses were used to explore Antarctica. These Manchurian horses
accompanied Sir Ernest Shackleton and were fed on a meat-based diet
created by the British army.*

Additionally, he wrote, "compared to the dog, the pony is a far more
efficient animal, one pony doing the work of at least ten dogs and travelling a further distance in a day...... It was trying work for the ponies
but they all did splendidly in their own particular way."
(*Lieutenant Shackleton's Own Story* by Sir Ernest Shackleton,
Pearson's magazine, 1909.)

The harsh weather and unforgiving terrain caused the men and
horses to struggle alike through the cold and snow, but Shackleton
made a startling observation. The horses preferred to eat the meat-based
ration rather than the traditional fodder. They even threw corn out of
their nosebags, scattering it on the ground, in anger at being denied the
Maujee ration.

On November 6, 1908, Shackleton first noted, "They all like the
Maujee ration and eat that up before touching their maize."

A few days later, both men and horses had begun taking special
notice of the meat-filled horse food. On November 9, Shackleton wrote,

"Tonight we boiled some Maujee ration for the ponies, and they took this feed well. It has a delicious smell and we ourselves would have enjoyed it."

By the end of the month one of Shackleton's horses, Quan, was "disgusted at not having more Maujee ration and flings his maize out of his nosebag."

Because of the dangers and hardships of the journey, three of the gallant horses had to be put down on the outward journey, but Shackleton, his men and the remaining horse, Socks, pressed ever onward towards the South Pole.

On December 3, 1908, at 7 p.m., Sir Ernest Shackleton, his three human companions, and their sole remaining pony, Socks, pitched camp – and made history.

Socks the Manchurian pony holds a special place in equestrian history for two reasons. No other horse ever came as close to reaching the South Pole and he is the first recorded horse to have shared a meat-based meal with his master.

Because the four men and the sole surviving horse were "tired and hungry, we made a good dinner which included a cupful of Maujee ration as an extra."

By sharing the Maujee ration, Shackleton and Socks became the first known horse and human to consume meat together.

Sadly, neither Shackleton nor Socks gained the South Pole. On December 7, Socks fell into a "black bottomless pit." Had Socks not died, a meat-eating horse may well have helped Shackleton reach the South Pole.

Shackleton and his men marched on for an additional month, coming remarkably close to their elusive geographic goal. He had, however, opened the door to a remarkable series of events – a dual equestrian exploration of Antarctica by Great Britain and Germany, both of which also employed meat-eating horses.

Unlikely Equestrian Allies

Sadly, due to a variety of factors, including the onset of motorized transportation, today there is a global lack of knowledge regarding the history of equestrian travel. For at least six thousand years brave men and women had been climbing onto horses and setting off in search of adventure and freedom. Yet despite being mankind's oldest link with the horse, this timeless equestrian legacy and its attendant accumulated knowledge have nearly disappeared, not just from the market place, but from all human memory.

An excellent example of this can be found in the common belief that the race for the South Pole only involved Norway and England.

Modern folklore delights in focusing on the intense rivalry which existed between the Norwegians, led by Roald Amundsen, and the English, led by Captain Robert Scott, with the former relying on dogs to pull their sleds, while the latter obstinately preferred to "man haul" their equipment across the ice. That story sold reams of newspapers in its day and continues to fuel a lucrative niche publishing industry today. This is an erroneous simplification of events perpetrated by pedestrians, one which overlooks an astonishing series of under-reported equestrian events.

Disregarded is the fact that this was not a two-horse race between two bitter nationalistic foes determined to champion different methods of travel. Prior to Scott's departure for Antarctica, Germany and England were still on such friendly terms that it was agreed their explorers would simultaneously use horses, some of whom it was later discovered were meat-eaters, to try and meet each other in Antarctica.

This decision was brought about in 1912, when Germany's Kaiser Wilhelm II authorized explorer Wilhelm Filchner to travel to the South Pole. The young German had already made successful explorations across Central Asia, most notably when he rode from Baku to the Pamir Mountains in the late 19th century.

Having received his nation's commission to explore the southern-most continent, Filchner journeyed to London in search of first-hand knowledge regarding polar travel. Here he was befriended by Captain Robert Scott and Sir Ernest Shackleton, both of whom encouraged and helped the amateur Polar explorer.

After a series of meetings it was agreed that somewhere in the vast white expanse of Antarctica, the Germans, led by Filchner, would locate the British team, led by Captain Scott, whereupon the two nations would exchange personnel before retiring to their respective camps on either side of the continent. Both expeditions were to use horses, in addition to sled dogs. The British also relied upon motor-driven tractors, and in extremis, man-hauling.

Neither team leader realized at the time that both their expeditions would unknowingly rely on meat-eating equines in this effort. Nor was it known that the Norwegians were even planning on being anywhere near Antarctica, as Amundsen had announced he was trying instead for the North Pole. Therefore, if events had gone as planned, German and English equestrian travellers would have met as friends somewhere in the vast frozen continent.

Sadly, this did not occur. Filchner's role was air brushed out of popular history. Germany's involvement was ignored, as it distracted from the unexpected rivalry brought about by Norway's explorer showing up to thwart Scott's role. Nor were the equestrian events, either before or after Scott's death, fully understood or documented.

To begin with, a lucrative modern industry has arisen which delights in highlighting the personal and professional dispute which had arisen between Scott and his former lieutenant, Shackleton. All too often it is forgotten that on their first expedition to Antarctica, Scott had saved Shackleton's life.

Consequently, while they were indeed rivals for the Pole, what the opponents of either camp neglect to appreciate is that both men maintained an abiding respect for each other's talents.

Moreover, thanks to Filchner's unexpected appearance in London, a significant moment in equestrian travel history soon occurred. This came about when Scott was preparing to leave England's capital. His slow ship and her crew had already departed for Antarctica. Having concluded last-minute fund-raising, Scott was now taking a train to the coast. There he would board a fast sailing passenger liner bound for New Zealand, where he would rendezvous with his expedition.

When Scott boarded the train, Shackleton and Filchner were waiting to bid their fellow explorer farewell.

Thus, Shackleton and Scott, the two former expedition comrades, shared a poignant final meeting. Any residual antagonism which existed between the Irish and English explorers was temporarily laid to rest, as the two experienced polar travellers expressed what were unknowingly going to be their last farewells.

Ironically, as the train pulled out of the station, Scott's final words were aimed not at Shackleton, with whom he had shared many desperate adventures, but at his fellow equestrian explorer, Wilhelm Filchner.

"See you at the South Pole," Scott yelled to Filchner, as the train pulled away from the London station.

As Scott departed, none of the three explorers could have realized that this was their last meeting. The lure of the South Pole would soon kill Scott. It would then seriously imperil the lives of Filchner, Shackleton and all the men involved in both their own expeditions.

South Pole Ponies

What is seldom remembered today is that, like Shackleton and Jackson before them, Filchner and Scott were also using Siberian and Manchurian horses to assist them in their push to the frozen end of the Earth.

Upon departing from London, Filchner returned to Germany, convinced that he and Scott were in agreement on an extraordinary plan which incorporated the themes of international cooperation, scientific advancement and horses. There had been no hint of commercial, national or personal competition.

Filchner never met Scott. Paradoxically, he encountered his nemesis instead.

After setting sail for Antarctica with his ship and crew, the German stopped at the harbour of Buenos Aires. There Filchner chanced upon the *Fram*. This was the Norwegian ship captained by that country's famous polar explorer, Roald Amundsen. Unknown to Scott, this Norwegian rival had unexpectedly launched what was to become a nationalistic race to the South Pole. The *Fram*, with Amundsen's large contingent of sled dogs, sailed first. Afterwards, Filchner and his German expeditionary force also departed for Antarctica, bound for the opposite side of the continent than that which the Norwegian and British expeditions had chosen.

Like Scott, prior to his departure Filchner had purchased Manchurian horses to explore Antarctica. Like Amundsen, Filchner also brought dogs too. Upon arriving, he was surprised to learn that, because the dogs viewed the ship as a home, they had to be separated by force from the ship, unlike the horses who eagerly went ashore and "when they felt terra firma under their hooves; they bit, kicked and pranced from high spirits and joie-de-vivre."

Filchner also remarked on the ease which his horses pulled sledges weighing 1,200 pounds.

"As draught animals the ponies achieved miracles."

Though the Germans were unable to either reach the South Pole, or locate Scott, they enthusiastically rode them in Antarctica. One German, the Historical Long Rider, Alfred Kling, regularly explored on a Manchurian horse named Moritz. Another of these horses, Stasi, eagerly ate dried fish and raw seal-meat.

Though three Antarctic expeditions used meat-eating horses, recent books have continued to denigrate and erase this portion of equestrian history. One volume states, "No horse that set foot on Antarctic ground ever returned."

(*Antarctic Destinies* by Stephanie Barczewski, published by Continuum Books, London, 2007.)

Meat-eating horses, such as the one ridden by the German Antarctic explorer, Alfred Kling, were used by the Kaiser's expedition to the South Pole.

This statement is misleading, if not inaccurate, because even though the German expedition was unable to proceed off the ice and onto terra firma, upon the completion of his journey to Antarctica German Long Rider Wilhelm Filchner did indeed save all of his horses. He released the still-healthy Manchurian horses on South Georgia Island, allowing them to run wild on the Hestesletten (Horse Plain). The descendants of these horses remained on the island for decades.

(*To the Sixth Continent, the Second German South Polar Expedition* by Wilhelm Filchner. Published by Ullstein Verlag, Berlin, 1922.)

While Filchner had problems, Scott was facing a disaster on the other side of the continent.

Apsley Cherry-Garrard was one of the youngest members of Captain Scott's final expedition to Antarctica. His book, *The Worst*

Journey in the World, is the gripping account of how Scott's expedition went wrong.

The Englishman's prototype motorized transport broke down. The weather was appalling, even by Antarctic standards. Some of his horses were lost in accidents. His men lacked experience skiing or driving dogs.

Nevertheless, Cherry-Garrard recalled how Scott's men cheerfully travelled for science, doing hard work "without any thought of personal gain."

Despite the horrors that Scott and his men eventually faced, Cherry-Garrard's account includes numerous clues to Antarctica's forgotten equestrian past.

For example, the doughty Englishmen sang as they marched alongside their ponies over the ice towards the distant South Pole. The singing may have been an attempt to cheer themselves up, because three of the horses had the unenviable reputation of being "man-eaters." The worst of these was Christopher. He was described as being "very dangerous, savage" and "a man killer if ever there was; he had to be thrown in order to attach him to the sled."

Unlike Jackson and Shackleton, Scott took a different view on equine nutrition. He brought none of the high-energy Maujee ration for his horses, deciding instead to feed them compressed fodder made of wheat. He also gave the horses hot bran mash with either oats or oil-cake on alternate days.

Despite their traditional diet of hay, oats, bran and oil cake, the equestrian report compiled after the English expedition concluded, "The nutritive value was insufficient under the conditions of sledging and the ponies became very weak and lost flesh markedly. So much so that in the ration for the Southern Journey, a large proportion of oats and oil cake were incorporated. The total weight of the daily ration of these feeds was 11 pounds per pony per day. It was increased to 13 pounds per day and was still insufficient."
(*Notes on the Ponies and Mules used during the Terra Nova expedition of 1910-12* by E.L. Atkinson)

Regardless of his well-meaning efforts, Scott's horses "lost weight until they were just skin and bone."

Even though they lacked the tasty Maujee ration, eyewitnesses recorded that at least one of Scott's horses was an avid meat-eater.

"One of our ponies, Snippets, would eat blubber and so far as I know it agreed with him," Cherry-Garrard wrote.
(*The Worst Journey in the World: The Story of Scott's Last Expedition to the South Pole* by Apsley Cherry-Garrard, published by Pimlico & Co, London, 1922.)

Despite their worthy goals, Scott and four of his men reached the South Pole a month after Amundsen and the Norwegians had arrived there. Due to severe weather and diminishing supplies, the five disappointed Englishmen died on the return journey.

Snippets, the meat-eating horse who Captain Scott led on his journey across Antarctica.

While Amundsen had been obsessed with the goal of being first to the South Pole, Cherry-Garrard believed Scott's men symbolized an alternative view, the conquest of self, of one's "interior pole."

"They were prepared to suffer great hardship and some them died for their beliefs."

Cherry-Garrard was later part of the rescue party that found the frozen bodies of Scott and two of the men who had accompanied him on the final push to the Pole. Once again, the equestrian portion of that tale has been almost entirely deleted from popular cultural records.

Prior to his fatal departure to the South Pole, Scott had written to the British army authorities in India asking them to authorize the use of mules which had been specially trained in the Himalayan mountains. In accordance with that request, seven of these carefully trained mules travelled from India, down to New Zealand, and on to Antarctica. Accompanying them was special equipment based on ideas formulated in the Tibetan Himalayas. This included equine snow shoes and tinted snow goggles.

These valuable animals accompanied the rescue party, led by the surgeon Dr. Edward Atkinson, which set out to locate Scott and his missing men. The snow shoes sent from India worked so well that the mules were able to cross crevasses with them.

In a special equestrian report later authored by Atkinson, he stated that "the mules covered nearly 400 miles and were in such good fettle they could have done it again…..They were obviously stronger and better trained than the ponies and would have done even better than the ponies and pulled longer distances."

Nevertheless, Atkinson noted that when it came time for the English expedition to leave Antarctica, the perfectly healthy mules were killed rather than being returned to either New Zealand or India.

(*Notes on the Ponies and Mules used during the Terra Nova expedition of 1910-12* by E.L. Atkinson)

The facts disclosed in this portion of the LRG-AF study are a memorial to the equines that deserve credit for their contributions to human efforts to explore our world. This includes examples of the O'Reilly Anomaly which occurred in the Arctic Circle and Antarctica. In spite of that there is still an entrenched dog-friendly view of polar history which has been written by those lacking any appreciation or understanding of equestrian history.

A striking example of this antagonistic philosophy is provided by *The Antarctic Dictionary, A complete guide to Antarctic English*. Authored by Bernadette Hince, and published in 2000 by CSIRO

Publishing, this so-called "complete guide" has no mention of horses, ponies or mules. There are a total of 394 pages, most of which consist of quotations from various books on the subject, yet the author has eliminated equestrian events, and any reference to meat-eating horses, out of her dictionary.

With the death of Captain Scott, and the failure by the Germans to reach the South Pole, the curtain drew down on the role of meat-eating horses in Polar exploration history; yet astonishing episodes were occurring further north.

There the LRG-AF made an incredible discovery. Horses in Central Asia, it was learned, eagerly devoured raw equine liver and other sources of meat, while once again assisting explorers from the Edwardian age.

Tales of Tibet

First the Guild confirmed that the Historical Swedish Long Rider, Sven Hedin, had noted in the late 19th century how the nomadic Hor-pa tribe of Tibet nourished their horses on meat mixed with ground barley.

The Hor-pa nomads were descended from Mongol soldiers sent by Kublai Khan to set up post stations. After the collapse of the Mongol empire, the Hor soldiers remained in Tibet. It was their routine practice in winter, when snow covered the grazing, to nourish their ponies with dried or powdered meat, tsampa (puffed and ground barley), and tea. (*Yugur Ethnonyms* by Mavi Boncuk, June 27, 2004.)

On his two-year journey through the remote highlands of Tibet, Hedin reported, "The two small Tibetan horses, which travel with us, take a great interest in the horses we rode here from India; but they do not seem quite sure that our animals, which are so thin and wretched, are really horses. At this day's camp, No. 63, the Tibetan horses ran up to their masters for two large pieces of frozen antelope flesh, which they eagerly ate out of their hands like bread. They are just as fond of yak or sheep's flesh, and the Tibetans say that this diet makes them tough and hardy. We cannot help liking these small shaggy ponies, which live to no small extent on the offal of game, are at home in the mountains, and tolerate rarefied air with the greatest ease. The cold does not trouble them in the least; they remain out all through the night without a covering of any sort, and even a temperature of - 22.7 Celsius (- 4 Fahrenheit), does not affect them. Though they are not shod, they run deftly and securely up and down the slopes, and the men on their backs look bigger than their horses."

The next month, January, Hedin made this observation about the ability of the Tibetan ponies to maintain condition as opposed to the down-country horses from Ladakh.

"We knew we had a trying way before us, and therefore we made an early start. The Ladakhi horse that bore the number 22 on the label attached to his mane lay frozen hard before my tent, with his legs stretched out; he had served us faithfully for nearly half a year. Seven horses and a mule were left alive in our caravan. They carried nothing but the cloths that protected them from cold in the night. Yet the new Tibetan horses were in splendid condition; they were fat and sleek compared with our old horses."

(*Trans-Himalaya: Discoveries and Adventures in Tibet* by Sven Hedin, MacMillan Publishers, London, 1909)

But it was the detailed eyewitness notes made by the French Long Rider Gabriel Bonvalot which surprised the Guild, as Bonvalot had not only witnessed such meat-eating horses, he had also ridden them!

The annals of the Historical Long Riders include men and women of astounding bravery, remarkable resourcefulness and enduring optimism. Then there is Gabriel Bonvalot, whose remarkable rides "through the Heart of Asia" mark him as the most influential French Long Rider of the 19th century.

Bonvalot (1853-1933) was a French explorer, author, and legislator whose exploits in the saddle began in 1880 when he set out to explore Central Asia. Accompanied by the noted French scientist, Dr. Guillaume Capus, the fearless French Long Riders explored the fabled kingdoms of Bukhara, Khiva and Samarqand. A few years later they once again rode across Central Asia, then turning southward, tried to penetrate into the hostile kingdom of Afghanistan. They were seized, imprisoned and then expelled back towards Samarqand. Refusing to concede defeat, Bonvalot determined to reach India via an obscure caravan track which reputedly ran across the Pamir and Hindu Kush mountains.

According to legend, this "Roof of the World" had been created when the Devil lifted the entangled mass of 20,000 foot high mountains to see what mysteries lay underneath. After a perilous winter passage, the Frenchmen managed to reach the remote mountain kingdom of Chitral. Instead of being hospitably received, they were again imprisoned as trespassers but, with the help of sympathetic British authorities, were eventually released and allowed to travel on to India. These daring expeditions placed Bonvalot alongside the ranks of the English explorer Younghusband, the Russian explorer Prejevalsky and the Swedish explorer Hedin.

Yet those two journeys could be considered "training trips" for what came next.

In 1889 Bonvalot set out to make an unparalleled journey of 9,500 kilometres from France to French Indochina, with most of the journey being made on horseback. Accompanying the seasoned equestrian explorer this time was Prince Henri d'Orléans, a young aristocrat with a craving for adventure and a talent for photography. After crossing Russia, the Frenchmen mounted up in Siberia, and headed south towards Tibet. The resultant equestrian winter journey across the Tibetan plain and the Himalayan mountains is nearly too arduous to believe. The men routinely rode in weather so cold that their Siberian companions begged them to turn back when the mercury in the thermometer froze.

Yet Bonvalot's courage and resistance overcame all obstacles. "Our diet is always the same," he wrote. "The frozen meat we chop with an axe. Our water is always dirty because it comes from melting ice. Tea never really boils on account of the altitude. The dust, mud, sand and hairs from our furs and beasts which we find in our food, are things which we have long ceased to pay attention to."

In an English translation detailing how he rode from Siberia towards Lhasa, Bonvalot recalled how on March 7th, 1891 he obtained and rode meat-eating horses in Tibet.

"We have had some small Tibetan horses given us which are full of go, and which feed on raw flesh, as we have seen with our own eyes. These carnivorous beasts have marvellous legs, and are as clever as acrobats; they balance themselves with the greatest care on the ice or amid dirty bogs, and then, gaining the path with a bound, carry us along at a rapid trot, to which we have long been unaccustomed. Anyone

would imagine that they find us to be as light as feathers, and we certainly look far more like lean hermits than fat monks."
(*Across Thibet – Being a Translation of De Paris au Tonking* by Gabriel Bonvalot, Cassell Publishing, New York, 1892.)

During his extraordinary journey from Paris to Tonkin, French Historical Long Rider Gabriel Bonvalot had nothing but praise for the meat-eating horses he rode in Tibet.

Defying Nature

It isn't easy to demystify nature, especially when the evidence contradicts what we previously believed.

A case in point is King Kong, the gigantic prehistoric gorilla invented for the cinema by Merian C. Cooper.

Before he became a famous Hollywood film maker, Cooper was a Historical Long Rider whose mounted journey across Persia with the

Bakhtiari nomads resulted in an important documentary. That 1920s ride required Cooper to cross raging rivers, ride over ice-covered peaks and deal with the reality of nature.
(*www.milestonefilms.com/movie.php/grass/*)

In stark contrast, though he captured our imaginations, Cooper's 1930s fictional monster, King Kong, defied nature.

According to palaeontologist and evolutionary biologist, Professor Stephen Jay Gould, creatures such as King Kong cannot exist.

"The forms and behaviors that living organisms show, and that we study with such fascination, are multiply determined. In the first place, there are rules of structure. Despite the movie makers, an ape the size of King Kong is impossible; its bones would crumble under its own weight."
(*www.nytimes.com/books/97/11/09/home/gould-teeth.html*)

When *King Kong* was released in 1933 the eyes of the movie-going public were deceived into contemplating the existence of a mythical gorilla who could scale the Empire State Building.

That was a mirage.

What German explorers found in Tibet also defied common belief, but the existence of blood-eating horses was real.

Into Tibet

In 1938 one of the 20th century's most controversial scientific expeditions ventured into Tibet. It was led by Dr. Ernst Schäfer, a renowned scientist, courageous explorer and member of the Nazi party.

It is the latter which has doggedly overshadowed Schäfer's other accomplishments, including the fact that he alone filmed a Tibetan horse consuming blood tsampa.

Like Cooper, Schäfer also had links to equestrian travel. As a child, he had been inspired to become an explorer by Wilhelm Filchner, the Historical Long Rider who had employed meat-eating horses in Antarctica. As a promising young scholar, Schäfer accompanied two specimen-gathering expeditions led by the wealthy American naturalist, Brooke Dolan, for the Academy of Natural Sciences of Philadelphia.

When the Second World War erupted, Dolan made an extraordinary equestrian journey from India across Tibet and into China. The naturalist turned soldier was charged with carrying secret diplomatic greetings and gifts from President Franklin Roosevelt to the young Dalai Lama.
(*www.thelongridersguild.com/tolstoy1.htm*)

But in the pre-war days of the early 1930s Dolan and Schäfer travelled into eastern Tibet in search of scientific truth, not clandestine alliances. On the second of these journeys, Schäfer debunked the myth of the yeti, demonstrating that the tracks previously attributed to the "abominable snowman," were actually made by a Tibetan bear.
(*Schäfer biography by Jorge Gonzalez - www.michael-polster.de/wp-content/uploads/2010/11/Gonzalez-2010-Schafer.pdf*)

Upon his return to Germany in 1935, Schäfer's articles and books attracted the attention of one of the most notorious men in history, Heinrich Himmler, Reichsführer of the SS.

Mixed Messages

Because its scientific accomplishments were overshadowed by speculation regarding Nazi occultism, Schäfer's 1938 expedition to Tibet has been forgotten by many and misunderstood by most. Science collided with superstition when Schäfer's expedition was influenced by Himmler's politics.

The reason for this confusion is linked to the Reichsführer's fascination with mysticism and pseudo-scientific theories, some of which were connected to Tibet. In an effort to use Schäfer for propaganda purposes, and to confirm Nazi mythology, Himmler offered financial and logistical support. But there were strings attached to this Faustian offer.
(*http://en.wikipedia.org/wiki/1938%E2%80%931939_German_expedition_to_Tibet*)

Fearing that his academic credentials would be compromised, Schäfer refused to allow a proponent of Himmler's theories to accompany the expedition. He also insisted on being granted scientific freedom, although Schäfer, and the four young scientists who were to accompany him, were required to be members of the SS.

Ironically, after receiving political advice from the famous British explorer, Sir Francis Younghusband, Schäfer went on to raise 80% of the funds from private sources, including his old friend Brook Dolan. The major financial contribution from Himmler was to arrange for the expedition's flight home to Germany.

Despite Himmler's limited patronage, Schäfer denounced the "worthless goings-on" of a whole army of quacks who associated Tibet with Nazi superstitions.
(*http://en.wikipedia.org/wiki/Nazism_and_occultism*)

He focused instead on collecting rare Buddhist books, visiting Lhasa, conducting geomagnetic experiments and overseeing the taking of more than 60,000 photographs which depict Tibet before the Chinese invasion.

The result was that Schäfer's multidisciplinary expedition was able to investigate Tibet with a level of detail previously unachieved by other European expeditions.
(*Tibet in 1938-1939, Photographs from the Ernst Schäfer Expedition to Tibet* by Isrun Engelhardt, Serindia Publications, 2007)

Schäfer also made a film which recorded a shocking equestrian event: a Tibetan horse consuming a special blood-based meal.

Arrow Riders

After escaping from the Apaches, John Cremony restored his horse's health by feeding it raw steak. Though that ride, known as the "Journey of Death," had occurred in New Mexico in 1851, less than a hundred years later Dr. Ernst Schäfer witnessed a strangely similar incident on the roof of the world.

Only this time the horse and rider weren't outrunning an enemy across the desert, they were riding over the world's highest mountains, and instead of steak at the end of the trail, it was hot blood and tsampa.

Schäfer's documentary, entitled *Geheimnis Tibet* (Secret Tibet), explains how an equestrian postal system kept Tibet connected to India. The idea of a mounted rider delivering important messages was nothing new. Genghis Khan established an imperial communication system called the *yam*, which employed "arrow riders" to communicate with the various portions of his far-flung empire, including Tibet.

Because the route crossed the Himalayan Mountains, only the strongest horses and mules were employed to carry the mail between northern India and southern Tibet. The result was that Tibetan post riders were still carrying the mail in relays, riding the 185 kilometres between Gyantse and Phari in only 24 hours.

Geheimnis Tibet records the arrival of one such rider at the village of Kalashar (Eastern Kala), on a plateau located nearly 5,000 metres (16,400 feet) above the sea.

In his diary, expedition anthropologist Bruno Beger recalled that the team had spent New Year's Day at Kalashar. They planned to depart for the next village of Samada on January 2, 1939 but bad weather delayed their departure until later that morning. While waiting for their horses to be made ready, the team witnessed the arrival of a Tibetan post rider.

According to the film's narrator, he is seen mounted on a tough native horse. Accompanying them is a hardy pack mule carrying a large wooden box marked "India Post Office." Once the mule is unloaded, the Germans are seen gratefully receiving letters from home. While the mule is allowed to roll in the dust, the weary horse is presented with a special meal designed to restore its strength before the return journey.

The Blood Tsampa

Although there are several notable examples of Europeans involved with meat-eating Tibetan horses, only Ernst Schäfer filmed the feeding of blood tsampa to a horse. The blood tsampa is clearly depicted between minutes 48 and 50 of *Geheimnis Tibet* and can be viewed on line. (*www.youtube.com/watch?v=Vmh4GLddGG8*)

Tsampa is made from roasted barley flour, mixed with yak butter and salty Tibetan tea. Simple to prepare, it was traditionally the main food of the nomads of Tibet. Not only is tsampa convenient and easily digestible, it also provides a rapid energy boost. (*http://en.wikipedia.org/wiki/Tsampa*)

Blood is rich in iron and can have a revitalizing effect. Mixing the tsampa with the blood was akin to placing a bitter pill in a spoonful of honey. The unorthodox result was a home-made, high-altitude equestrian pick-me-up.

Schäfer's documentary depicts a black sheep being slain according to Tibetan tradition. The animal was placed on its back and restrained. The butcher then cut its chest open, reached inside and severed the aorta. This caused rapid fatal internal bleeding, which filled the stomach with blood.

A Tibetan is seen scooping handfuls of blood out of the sheep's body and depositing the liquid into a large wooden bowl. The narrator explains that tsampa is also placed in the bowl. The horse is then led forward and allowed to consume this revitalizing meal.

Schäfer says the horse ate the blood tsampa "calmly".

Astonishing

Bruno Beger later wrote about witnessing the blood tsampa. In his book, *Mit der deutschen Tibetexpedition Ernst Schäfer 1938/39 nach Lhasa,* Beger noted how Ernst Krause, the expedition's cameraman and entomologist, wished to film the episode.

The anthropologist recalled how the expedition members were "astonished" when they observed the horse being fed the blood tsampa. Not only did the Tibetan horse show no aversion to eating the blood tsampa, according to Beger, the animal derived visible strength from consuming this powerful food.

"We were surprised. The animal showed no shyness and refreshed itself with visible enjoyment."

Yet the German explorer wondered, "How would our horses behave at home?"

During their 1938 expedition, Dr. Ernst Schäfer's team of German explorers created a unique documentary entitled Geheimnis Tibet (Secret Tibet).

The film depicts the arrival of a Tibetan post rider, who has carried the mail from India across the Himalayan mountains into southern Tibet.

The Germans were "astonished" to learn the Tibetans fed their weary horses a special revitalizing meal made from blood and tsampa. The first step in creating the high-energy food was to kill a sheep.

The sheep's blood was then scooped out by hand, placed in a wooden bowl and mixed with Tibetan tsampa.

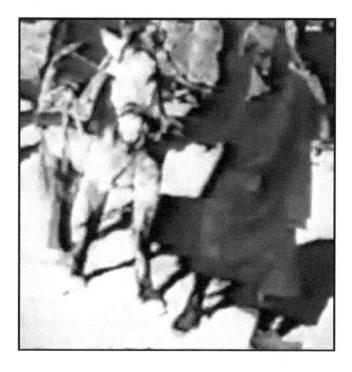

The film showed the post horse being led forward to his meal.

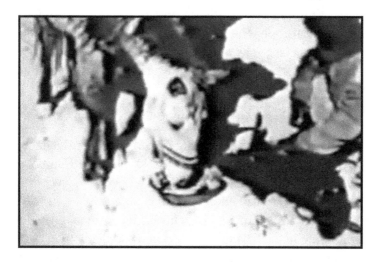

The Tibetan post horse dines on hot sheep blood and tsampa before beginning his return journey to India.

Modern Evidence

Though Schäfer and his German team-mates are the only westerners known so far to have seen the blood tsampa fed to a horse, modern academics have provided evidence of its existence.

Dr. Michel Peissel is a French ethnologist and explorer who has studied the horses of Tibet. In 1994 he documented the existence of the Nangchen, a miniature horse that has been raised in the Kham region of Tibet since the 9th century. The following year Peissel visited an isolated part of Tibet where he confirmed the existence of the Riwoche horse, an undiscovered breed described as a living fossil. Previously unknown in the West, Peissel believes these small Tibetan horses may provide an evolutionary link between prehistoric wild horses and modern domestic animals.
(*http://en.wikipedia.org/wiki/Michel_Peissel*)

When contacted by the Long Riders' Guild, the experienced Tibetan traveller said he had not witnessed horses eating blood tsampa. However in a scene reminiscent of Shackleton and Socks consuming the Maujee Ration together in Antarctica, Peissel confirmed Tibetan natives would also eat a mixture of blood and tsampa.

"The mixing of blood with tsampa is a staple food for some Tibetans when the opportunity arises," Peissel wrote. "Horses are Tibetans' most precious and often most expensive possessions. Nothing is too good for them. Dried yak meat is also often mixed with tsampa for horses to eat as a luxury."
(*Email to the Long Riders' Guild, June 4, 2011.*)

Additional evidence was provided by Professor Toni Huber. Writing from the Institut für Asien und Afrikawissenschaften at Humboldt University in Berlin, Huber said that though he had never witnessed the blood tsampa, Tibetans had informed him of similar evidence.

Dr. Huber is an anthropologist who has lived among the hunting nomads residing in the Changthang region of northern Tibet, a portion of the nation with very little vegetation. He recalled thinking the nomads were having fun at his expense when they told him their horses were fed blood, meat and offal.

"My informants reported that in the past they often fed their ponies with meat, animal offal and blood. At first I thought this was a joke played on me as a naïve foreign anthropologist. Then I came across a citation in one of Sven Hedin's accounts of the same area from the early 20th century," Huber wrote to the Guild.
(*Email to the Long Riders' Guild, June 7, 2011.*)

When the Guild asked Dr. Huber if he had witnessed the blood tsampa being fed to horses, he replied in the negative.

"This was not, to my knowledge, done in the northern Changthang areas I have worked in due to the scarcity of tsampa as a food staple. As Hedin's short report attests, what I was told was that horses were fed meat, fat and offal from various common game animal species, including Tibetan antelope, Tibetan gazelle, Tibetan wild ass, and one mention of wild yak meat."

It is also of interest to note that Dr. Huber may have discovered when the practice of raising meat-eating horses ceased in Tibet.

"The practice was not in evidence in my research area. The last mention of it being done was during the 1970s during times of food shortages under the Chinese imposed Commune system of collectivisation," he recalled.

What Dr. Huber was certain of was that the Tibetans had balanced the needs of their horses against the slim dietary options available on the cold Tibetan plateau. The result was a unique equestrian culture.

"Tibetans feeding horses parts of other animals is a good practical strategy since the horses do take this type of food, and a positive option for horses themselves in a vegetation poor area. The more interesting issue is whether this dietary strategy, which in the Tibetan examples I know of is clearly about a human-animal relationship, is one completely specific to the domestication relationship between horse and human?"

Dr. Huber concluded by saying he believed the discovery that Tibetan horses could consume blood tsampa and meat indicated that adaptability is the key to success for any species.

From Myth to Reality

Discovery of the blood tsampa is significant on many levels.

First, this was not a case of giving meat in an emergency, i.e. the "eat or die" situation Socks encountered in Antarctica. This was instead a case where both man and horse recognized the strength-giving properties which could be gained by voluntarily consuming the blood tsampa.

Moreover, discovery of the *Geheimnis Tibet* film moved the concept of meat-eating horses from the realm of ancient Greek mythology into the modern world of cinema.

The Tibetan evidence would also appear to lay to rest the popular idea that horses are herbivores. This eager consumption of blood would indicate that they are, and always have been, omnivores.

Also, because of Britain's long connections with Tibet, it raised an interesting question. Could the inspiration for Shackleton's Maujee Ration lie in Tibet? If so then Antarctic exploration history had a previously unknown link to "the roof of the world."

Though the First and Second World Wars occurred during the next few decades, the concept of raising meat-eating horses was still being practised in Tibet at the dawn of the Nuclear Age.

The first clue came in 1949.

Scottish Long Rider George Patterson is famous for having ridden across the Himalayas in the winter of 1950 to bring word to the outside world that Tibet had been invaded by the communist Chinese. But before leaving Tibet, where he had lived for several years, George also observed meat-eating equines.
(*www.thelongridersguild.com/Patterson-Story.htm*)

In a special interview with the LRG-AF, Patterson said, "As I recall it was a fairly accepted practice with special horses. For example, my Khampa chieftain friend, Topgyay Pangdatshang, had a favourite pacing mule that was fed chopped meat mixed with grain. I never gave this practice a thought until I was forced to enter a race against a Tibetan bandit chief. Ordinarily, Tibetans used a mixture of cold brick tea and yak butter to prime their horses for racing. But knowing my crafty opponent, before the race started I taunted him by asking if he had

cheated by priming his horse with a mixture of grain, meat and a Szechwan favourite spice of crushed walnut, oil and peppers."
(*Email to the Long Riders' Guild – July 28, 2007*)

Though Patterson was involved in a sporting event, other Long Riders were soon racing for their lives on meat-eating horses.

While Bonvalot and Hedin's accounts were amazing, more surprising was the discovery that there were still-living Long Riders who had ridden meat-eating horses.

Ride or Die

In the spring of 1950 Vasili Zvansov, a Russian refugee living in Tihwa, China, had to flee the oncoming Chinese communist army. Vasili joined a caravan headed by the American Consul, Douglas MacKiernan. Also along for the ride was an American academic, Frank Bessac, who had been trapped while studying in Mongolia. Their plan was to escape on horseback across the deserts of Western China, over the Himalayas and on to the safety of faraway Lhasa, Tibet.

Having initially eluded their Chinese pursuers, when the equestrian escapees reached the desert, Kazakh nomads advised the travellers that, because there was no pasture ahead, they could only proceed if they rode specially-trained, meat-eating horses. The Kazakh chief, Hussein Taiji, said that such horses were rare, and would cost twice as much.

The diet of these extraordinary horses was another equine, the wild ass of Central Asia.

"The kyangs or wild asses of the steppe could also be seen by the thousand. They lived in smaller herds than the yaks: each herd consisted of one stallion with a harem of from ten to fifty mares. When they ran, they ran like arrows, light brown on their backs and pale-coloured on their bellies, with long thin almost-black tails; they stretched out their necks and their tails streamed behind them, and they were a magnificent sight. The autumn was their rutting season. They were very curious and often surrounded the caravan, neighing at the caravan-animals and sometimes goading the pack beasts into flinging off their loads and galloping off after them. Some of the pack animals ran off with the kyangs and were never seen again, their packs lost forever as well," one European explorer reported.

Mounted on the meat-eating horses trained by the Kazakhs, the Russian and Americans set out to ride along a route never before travelled by foreigners.

(*www.thelongridersguild.com/bessac.htm*)

Thomas Laird, author of *Into Tibet: The CIA's First Atomic Spy and His Secret Expedition to Lhasa*, tracked down Zvansov and Bessec, the last two survivors of that extraordinary escape and shared his findings with the Guild. Even though they had lost contact with each other during the intervening decades, both men told Laird the same tale.

Vasili reported, "We searched for three months amongst the Kazaks for these rare meat-eating horses. But when we found them we discovered they wouldn't eat just any kind of meat – they would only eat the liver of the wild ass, known as the Gobi Kulan. We also learned we couldn't feed them liver every day, or it would have killed them, so we fed them every few days. There was indeed no grass on the entire trip and only the horses which ate the liver survived the trip."

With the recent death of North American Long Rider Frank Bessac,
Russian émigré Vasili Zvansov is the last known person alive who rode,
and fed, meat-eating horses.

The Russian also told Laird that when they reported the existence of these meat-eating horses upon their return to the West, they were not believed. Yet even more dramatic evidence was soon provided from a far more famous source.

National Geographic Reports on Meat-Eating Horses

Shortly after Bessec and Zvansov escaped, the nomadic Kazakh tribe which raised these meat-eating horses also fled from the advancing Chinese communist army towards the safety of India. The Kazakhs too rode across the grassless deserts of Central Asia mounted on horses which could be fed on meat obtained en route.

This escape of an entire tribe was later documented by *National Geographic* magazine in their November, 1954 issue, who, though they specifically mentioned the meat-eating horses in their article, did not understand the global significance of what they had just printed.

Known as a deadly warrior and superb horseman, Kazakh chief Qali Beg led his tribe 3,000 miles from Sinkiang, China to safety in Kashmir, India. Part of the tribe's journey was done on specially trained meat-eating horses, who were able to survive in the grassless Takla Makan desert.

Dr. Milton Clark was the highly qualified expert who had documented this astonishing travel tale. Clark had served as a captain in northern China in the Second World War. In the 1950s he worked as a political analyst for the Department of Defence. A noted Harvard scholar, Clark spent a year among the Kazakh refugees who had reached Kashmir, recording their stories.

"My wiry, high-spirited hosts were the remnants of hordes of saddle-bred nomads who had fled the Communist regime which Red China had imposed on their native province of Sinkiang....I recognized the need to hear the survivors' own story of their fabulous migration."

What Clark discovered was that when communists attacked the main Kazakh camp, they killed or captured more than 12,000 tribesmen. The remnants fled into the mountains, all the while Communists continued to attack the mounted refugees. Only superb horsemanship and sharp shooting saved the dwindled remnants of the tribe.

As they made their way towards the safety of India, Clark wrote, their anxiety increased when they reached the eastern reach of the dreaded Takla Makan desert. Along this infamous route they saw the "bones of men and animals."

The National Geographic reporter noted, "The manna in the wilderness, however, was the small dun-coloured horse, known to the tribesmen as qulan. The Kazakhs hunted it from horseback, killing scores for the flavoursome, nourishing meat."

It was thanks to the flesh of these wild equines that the fleeing tribesmen noted how their horses gained "great strength" after being fed the qulan meat. After having survived seven attacks, the refugees reached the sanctuary of Kashmir in 1951. Forty-two Kazakhs and seventy-five horses had been lost during the long retreat.

(*How the Kazakhs Fled to Freedom* by Milton Clark, National Geographic Magazine – Volume CVI, Number Five, Page 637)

Considering that the topography of this area had not radically altered for thousand of years, the idea of feeding meat to horses in a grass-free zone had to be a long-standing tradition which had probably been used by generations of local horsemen. The Guild contacted Bessac prior to his death to discuss his experiences with meat-eating equines.

(*Death on the Chang Tang, Tibet, 1950: the Education of an Anthropologist* by Frank Bessac, University of Montana Press, 2006.)

When asked to comment on the Kazakh horses, the now retired professor of anthropology posed this question.

"It has occurred to me that this practice is doubtless of long standing. Could this custom have played a role in the successes of the armies of Genghis Khan and his Mongol cavalry riding over vast steppes?" (*Email to the Long Riders' Guild, August 17, 2007.*)

Mysteries of the Gobi

British explorer John Hare is an expert on the wild Bactrian camels who inhabit the Gobi desert in China and Mongolia. He founded the Wild Camel Protection Foundation of which Dr. Jane Goodall DBE is the Life Patron. Though his focus is on camels, Hare uncovered new information in 2010 about the meat-eating horses described by Bessac and National Geographic magazine.

The Kazakhs could still teach a horse to eat meat, and they offered to sell such an animal to the English explorer.

"On my recent trip I travelled with four Kazakhs, all of whom are related to the Kazakhs who completed the Gobi crossing. I asked them if they had had experience of flesh-eating horses and camels and they all confirmed they know how to train a horse/camel to eat flesh and if I would like to buy such a horse/camel they would start training it now."

The tribesmen informed Hare that this specialized training would take six months.

"There was absolutely no doubt in their minds that such an animal could be produced."
(*www.wildcamels.com*
Mysteries of the Gobi by John Hare, I. B Tauris & Co, 2009)

All the King's Horses

It might seem outlandish to think that an equestrian culture could still be riding meat-eating horses in the age of the internet. Yet Dr. Toni

Huber and John Hare uncovered evidence that knowledge of meat-eating horses had never disappeared among the Tibetans or Kazakhs.

Then a case of equestrian affinity was discovered in an adjacent country, one wherein similar cultural traditions were even now being practised.

Located at the eastern end of the mighty Himalayan mountains, horsemen living in the kingdom of Bhutan fed their horses a meal which resembles neighbouring Tibet's blood tsampa. In both cases a grain was mixed with animal protein.

Dorji Gyeltshen was Zimpon, or Lord Chamberlain, to His Majesty, Jigme Singye Wangchuck, the fourth king of Bhutan. In messages to the LRG-AF Gyeltshen explained how for thirty years he was responsible for the welfare of the forty horses owned by the king. The Lord Chamberlain said that during the winter, and especially after strenuous journeys, the royal horses were fed a special meal designed to restore their strength.

Instead of tsampa, the Bhutanese used a special flour called chie in Dzongkha, the national language of Bhutan. Rather than sheep's blood, the royal stable relied on fat collected from dead animals, including wild ones such as the tiger and bear.

While fat was also gathered from dead sheep, cattle or pigs, the tiger was deemed to be of special significance. Not only do the Bhutanese believe that its fat imparts great strength to the horse, the tiger is the horse's ally in the Bhutan zodiac. Regardless of which type of animal was chosen, the chie flour and fat were boiled together then fed to the horses.

According to the Lord Chamberlain, "the weak animals would recover faster and the healthy ones would become stronger. Plus, after eating the animal fat, the horses would have a lustre in their mane."
(*Email to the Long Riders' Guild, 3 June 2011*)

Another Bhutanese horseman, Tshewang Penjor, owns one of the largest herds of horses in the Paro valley. He informed the LRG-AF that he feeds his horses meat "when he can afford it." The most common choice is beef and yak, which is diced into small pieces and then mixed with grain or grass.

"The horses have no problem eating it," he reports.
(*Email to the Long Riders' Guild, 5 June 2011*)

As memories linger among the Tibetans and Kazakhs, evidence indicates that Bhutan still has a viable meat-eating horse culture.

But was the evidence restricted to the Orient? Could clues to this strange phenomenon be found among Occidental literature?

It didn't take the Guild long to follow a trail that led from Persia to Hollywood.

Shakespeare, Faulkner and Rowling

In June, 1940 the great detective, Hercule Poirot got it wrong. Writing in *The Strand* magazine, his creator Agatha Christie placed the fictional Belgian detective in a story entitled *The Horses of Diomedes*. Though Poirot was famous for using his "little grey cells" to solve every riddle, by the mid-20th century his authoress had apparently lost touch with the truth behind the story's title, as she credits the Belgian detective with saying that the murderous mares were merely "symbolic."

But other writers were more perceptive.

A meat-eating horse forms part of the creation myth of the Swahili people of eastern Africa. According to an 11th century legend a young man named Kibaraka, Little Blessing, rode a horse who could speak and eat meat.

"The horse spoke in clear language. 'Salaam aleikum, oh son of Adam'.....The horse said, "Now release the cattle.' Kibaraka opened the stable so that the cattle streamed out. The horse opened its mouth, and to the young man's great surprise, it swallowed them."
(*Myths and Legends of the Swahili* by Jan Knappert, Heinemann, Nairobi, Kenya in 1979.)

Another 11th century saga, the great Persian national epic entitled, the *Shahnama* (Book of Kings), told the tale of the legendary hero, Rustam, and his chestnut stallion Rakhsh. The mighty rose-coloured horse had been born in Afghanistan and allegedly had the strength of an elephant. Thanks to his intelligence and loyalty, Rakhsh played a significant part in Rustam's legendary travels.

During one of their many adventures, Rustam and Rakhsh set out on a long journey to rescue a king held captive by a demon. One night

they stopped to rest, not knowing that they had chosen to sleep near a lion's den. While Rustam slumbered, the lion attempted to attack the sleeping rider. Yet Rakhsh fought and killed the savage beast. Later the mighty stallion bit a dragon on the shoulder, distracting it so that Rustam was able to slay the monster.
(*http://en.wikipedia.org/wiki/Rakhsh*)

Persia is one of the many countries which have a legend about a horse so ferocious it could slay predators. In this tapestry, Rakhsh can be seen killing a lion. Horses are also known to have slain wolves, pumas, tigers and hyenas.

Centuries later, in faraway England, William Shakespeare incorporated meat-eating horses into his play, *Macbeth*. When Macbeth kills Duncan, the king of Scotland, the heavens and animals are so troubled by this bloody act that King Duncan's horses, the choicest of their breed, turn feral and eat each other.

"Duncan's horses (a thing most strange and certain)
Beauteous and swift, the minions of their race,
Turn'd wild in nature, broke their stalls, flung out,
Contending against obedience, as they would make
War with mankind."

One reviewer explains that in the medieval era the horse was believed to be the king who crowned the hierarchy of animals. Thus the actions taken by King Duncan's horses represent a collapse of nature's order.

By the time Queen Victoria was on the throne, British writer Mayne Reid wrote a remarkable account in 1856. It related how the now-extinct African equine, known as the quagga, mercilessly killed that notorious predator, the ferocious hyena.

"They were large animals – nearly of the size and shape of small horses – and travelling in single file; as they were, the troop at a distance presented something of the appearance of a caravan. There were in all about fifty individuals in the line; and they marched along with a steady sober pace; as if under the guidance and direction of some wise leader.

Ground coloured, tiger-like stripes upon their cheeks, neck and shoulders. Exactly of the same form as those upon a zebra; but less distinct, and not extending to the body or limbs, as is in the case of the true zebra. Though they had points in common with the horse, ass and zebra, they were distinct from any. To the zebra they bore the greatest resemblance, for they were in reality a species of zebra. They were quaggas.

The animal in question was browsing quietly along, and at length approached a small clump of bushes that stood out in the open ground. When close to the copse it was observed to make a sudden spring forward; and almost at the same instant, a shaggy creature leaped out of the bushes, and ran off. This last was no other than the ugly striped hyena. Instead of turning upon the quagga and showing fight, as one might have supposed so strong and fierce a brute would have done, the hyena uttered a howl of alarm, and ran off as fast as its legs would carry it.

They did not carry it far. It was evidently making for a larger tract of bush that grew near; but before it had got half-way across the open ground, the quagga came up behind, and uttering his shrill "couaag," reared forward and dropped with his fore-hoofs upon the hyena's neck. At the same time the neck of the carnivorous animal was clutched by the teeth and held as fast as if gripped by a vise. All looked to see the hyena free itself and run off again. They looked in vain. It never ran another yard. It never came alive out of the clutch of those terrible teeth. The quagga held his struggling victim with firm hold, began trampling it with his hoofs, and shaking it in his strong jaws, until in a few minutes the screams of the hyena ceased and his mangled carcass lay motionless upon the plain."

(*The Bush Boys* by Captain Mayne Reid, David Bogue, London, 1856)

The quagga's mastery over the carnivorous animal was so complete that frontier farmers in South Africa kept hyenas away from their cattle by bringing up with the herd a number of quaggas, who act as its guards and protectors.

Though modern mankind recognizes that the quagga became extinct in 1883, there will be many who struggle to believe in the continual existence of murderous equines.

Sceptics might argue that a vanished African equine, the quagga, does not provide adequate evidence of hyenas undergoing such an attack. Yet forty years later, in another corner of the British Empire, men and horses were indeed hunting hyenas together, according to a prominent London newspaper. Armed with spears, English huntsmen would set off to kill that despised predator. Even when the rider fell from the saddle, the horse voluntarily sought to kill the hyena.

Although hyenas were generally not fast enough to outrun horses, they had the habit of doubling and turning frequently during chases, thus ensuring long pursuits. This illustration entitled "The horse continues the chase" was published in the Illustrated London News on March 9, 1894 (page 195).
(*http://www.columbia.edu/itc/mealac/pritchett/00routesdata/1800_189 9/dailylife_drawings/ilnviews/hyenaspearing.jpg*)

A horse eagerly attempts to kill a hyena in India.

Further west, the noted European author, Franz Kafka, often used animals to symbolize how the bureaucratic world was attempting to suppress nature. As if he were writing to acknowledge a lingering European nightmare, in 1929 Kafka described nomads who were mounted on meat-eating horses.

In the short story entitled *An Old Manuscript* Kafka described how nomads, and their equally dangerous meat-eating horses, had been invited by the local emperor to take up residence within the walls of the frightened city.

"As is their nature, they camp under the open sky, for they abominate dwelling in houses. They busy themselves sharpening swords, whittling arrows and practising horsemanship..... As soon as the butcher brings in any meat the nomads snatch it all from him and gobble it up. Even their horses devour flesh; often enough a horseman, and his horse, are lying side by side, both of them gnawing at the same joint, one at either end."

(http://my.auburnjournal.com/detail/104668.html?content_source=&category_id=&search_filter=Emperor&user_id=&event_mode=&event_ts_from=&event_ts_to=&list_type=&order_by=&order_sort=&content_class=2&sub_type=&town_id=)

In 1969 the topic of meat-eating horses was an element in a Hollywood movie, starring Steve McQueen. The film was based upon William Faulkner's prize-winning novel

Yet these tales of meat-eating horses weren't restricted either to Europe or the past, because in 1969 one of Hollywood's greatest action heroes, Steve McQueen, starred in the film entitled *The Reivers*. Written in 1962 by the American novelist, William Faulkner, the Pulitzer Prize-winning book was set in 1910 Mississippi and told the tale of a race horse addicted to sardines.

(*The Reivers* by William Faulkner, Random House, New York, 1962.
The Reivers starring Steve McQueen, released in December, 1969.)

With Shakespeare and McQueen lurking in the literary background, is it any wonder J.K. Rowling decided to populate Harry Potter's magical world with carnivorous horses too? Various sources focus on the more pleasant ability of these creatures, which Rowling calls thestrals, to fly like Pegasus, while tending to neglect the literary roots linking them to meat-eating equines.

(*http://www.wisegeek.com/what-is-a-pegasus.htm*)

These legends, myths, stories, plays, books and movies clearly indicated that the practice of feeding flesh to horses was a long-standing planet-wide practice. But had evidence of the O'Reilly Anomaly disappeared, the Guild wondered?

The answer was, certainly not!

Modern Victims

On August 16, 1895 the *New York Times* reported that a "valuable and speedy stallion" nearly killed two attendants and attacked his owner, Thomas Edsall of Edenville, New York. "Mr. Edsall's arm was torn so badly as to render amputation necessary, and his head was badly lacerated. He is, perhaps, fatally injured."

This gruesome example has modern day counterparts as evidenced by three examples in a single year.

In 2009 an Indonesian man had his testicle bitten off by a cart horse.

"The 35-year-old was unloading sand from a horse-drawn cart at a construction site in Indonesia when the attack occurred. A witness said the animal suddenly lunged at the man in Sulawesi, sinking its teeth into him. As bystanders put the man in a car to take him to hospital, one noticed a piece of flesh on the pavement. "Luckily the horse did not chew up or swallow his testicle, but spit it onto the pavement," a witness said. It was not known whether doctors attempted to sew it back on. The owner explained that the horse, called Budi, was trained but sometimes turned wild, and had bitten in the past."

(*http://www.telegraph.co.uk/news/newstopics/howaboutthat/4983800/horse-bites-off-one-of-mans-testicles.html*)

In an eerie repeat of the "Man-Eater of Oudh," another horse in India ran amok and threatened the population of an entire town.

"A horse's reign of terror in the Indian state of Madhya Pradesh has residents living in fear, according to a local news report. India's Chronicle newspaper, in a story headlined 'Horse goes wild, bites people, many injured', reports at least 12 people "have fallen prey to the mad horse". The animal is reportedly "wandering amok at a gallop", causing panic among residents."
(*http://www.horsetalk.co.nz/news/2009/10/148.shtml*)

And a mustang stallion terrorized the Navajo reservation, forcing people to drive it off with gunfire.

"A rogue mustang was prowling the area, attacking anyone who ventured too near. We all laughed at the idea of a predatory horse. We definitely weren't laughing the next morning....I wheeled around, and the mustang shuddered to a stop, digging its hooves into the sand, its tail flicking in unmistakable anger. The horse and I were maybe 30 feet from one another, stuck in a sort of inter-species Mexican standoff. Finally, the animal pivoted and galloped away."
(*http://www.backpacker.com/december_07_destinations_over_the_rain bow_finding_red_rock_in_the_navajo_nation/destinations/12032*)

Nor did meat-eating equines disappear from the scene either.

In July, 2007 reporter Jason Wentworth contacted the Guild to describe a local couple who own meat-eating Icelandic horses in Alaska. "I just got off the telephone with Julie Collins, who writes the *Bush Life* feature for our local newspaper, the *Daily News-Miner*. She and her sister Mickey live out in the Alaska bush and live a subsistence hunting/trapping/fishing lifestyle with the help of their several Icelandic horses. The horses live free-range. When Mickey brings home a moose and tosses unusable parts out in the yard, the horses gnaw on them. The horses also lick up the blood from the spot where the couple slaughter their chickens."

Tales of horses devouring Alaskan moose raised an interesting question. Were ancient man, horse and dog all enthusiastic hunters? Did horses of old enjoy the kill and the meat? Before we could delve further into that possibility, other modern day examples of meat-eating horses emerged in Great Britain.

English Long Rider Richard Barnes was attending a fair at Herring-fleet in Suffolk, when, "a Dales stallion scooped up a Lapwing chick, feathers and all, and ate it, in front of an astonished crowd." Likewise Tanith Ellis in Scotland recalled how a donkey had killed and begun devouring a goat kid before her horrified family.
(*Emails to the Long Riders' Guild, September 10, 2006*)

And Welsh Long Rider Jeremy James reported that he had documented several cases where ponies and horses had devoured smaller animals in various parts of the UK.

"I too have witnessed this, when a Welsh pony I owned some years ago ripped up the body of a dead sheep. It was then that I thought about those wolf teeth and canines, and how a horse's defence mechanism is a kick and a bite."
(*Email to the Long Riders' Guild, October 17, 2002*)

Could there be a connection between the old adage, "the horse has the most inefficient digestive system in the world," and the possibility that the horse's stomach was created to digest meat, as well as grass and grain? Could horses have started out as omnivores?

Horses and History

There is an old joke about archaeologists which might shed an unexpected light on why mankind has misinterpreted the history of horses.

Upon discovering the remnant of a brick wall, buried eons ago, the excited archaeologist announced that the foot-high structure had originally been part of a massive temple complex, which was in turn connected to an ornate palace that had underground heating, an aviary and a view of the Tigris.

Mankind did the same thing with horses, only he built a tidy fantasy from a single tooth.

During the five years in which he made his famous scientific journey around the world, the Historical Long Rider, Charles Darwin, discovered the first fossil horse's tooth in Patagonia. After inspecting the artefact, Sir Richard Owen confirmed it belonged to an extinct

species named Equus curvidens. In 1841 Owen in turn discovered fossils of the earliest known horse. Because the skull was small, and the teeth did not resemble modern equine teeth, Owens concluded that the early equine might have been related to the pig, which does in fact have a stomach similar to a horse's. Owen subsequently named the animal Hyracotherium, meaning mole beast.
(*http://en.wikipedia.org/wiki/Sir_Richard_Owen*)

Owen's mole is more commonly known today as Eohippus, meaning dawn horse. This ancestral animal stood 12 inches high, had four hoofed toes and enjoyed a varied diet when it ran about 50 million years ago.
(*http://en.wikipedia.org/wiki/Evolution_of_the_horse*)

As other equine fossils were discovered, the horse became the best known example of a clear evolutionary progression. In order to demonstrate the logical sequence of evolution, transitional equine fossils were lined up left to right, starting with the tiny Eohippus, then progressing through the larger skeletons of Dinohippus, Epihippus and Mesohippus, until the display concluded with the recognizable skeleton of a large modern equine. This concept of little animals having ever bigger offspring was based upon the work of a 19th-century paleontologist named Edward Drinker Cope, who taught that within any group of animals there is a tendency for the descendants of a species to grow increasingly larger.

Until recently belief in what is known as "Cope's Law" stated that this steady sequence of ever-growing animals represented the single evolutionary pathway from which the modern horse developed. "Our modern horse is the direct descendant of a small animal which flourished 60 million years ago, called the Dawn Horse," states a modern book on equine evolution.

Scientists now realize this notion is incorrect. Modern horses did not evolve as the specific goal of ancient equids. In fact several species of ancestor horses might have co-existed, in a manner similar to that wherein Neanderthal and Cro-Magnon man also co-inhabited the planet.
(*http://www.flmnh.ufl.edu/sciencestories/2005/fossil_horses.htm*)

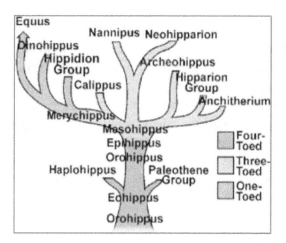

Though scientists previously believed horses evolved in a clear logical sequence, new evidence indicates that several prehistoric equines could have inhabited the planet simultaneously.

Just as the scientific concepts regarding the evolution of the horse's body size have changed, scientific questions should now be aimed at the horse's diet.

Horses, in fact, have a strange family history. They belong to the Perissodactyla order of animals which includes odd-toed ungulates that browse and graze, such as horses, tapirs and rhinoceroses. Horses digest their food in one stomach, rather than in several, as cows, camels and sheep do, with the equine digestive system making use of a single stomach, intestines, cecum and the colon, much like another omnivore, the human.

To further differentiate them, horses and mules have an enzyme which cattle lack. This enzyme breaks down and allows the horse to digest coarse cellulose. In unfortunate circumstances, horses are often able to survive harsh conditions on poor feed such as twigs, bark and dead grass.

And, we might ask, meat?

(http://www.sosrhino.org/news/rhinonews051305.php
http://en.wikipedia.org/wiki/Perissodactyla)

Teeth and Horses

In the days prior to mechanized transport, an old adage cautioned people to "never look a gift horse in the mouth." This warning was based upon the common practice of determining an animal's age by a careful study of its teeth, i.e. don't embarrass the giver by undertaking an overt dental examination demonstrating that the gift horse was actually an elderly member of the equine race.

Yet it is inside the horse's mouth that exciting scientific discoveries have rewritten our understanding of the horse's evolutionary history and long-term dietary habits.

Thanks to one of these new studies, we now know that the evolutionary path of horses is laid out in the fossil record of their teeth. Though dental changes lagged far behind alterations in the equine diet, they were brought about by the food available to prehistoric horses.

Two anatomy professors at New York College of Osteopathic Medicine (NYCOM) at the New York Institute of Technology examined the teeth of 6500 fossil horses. The teeth spanned a period of 55 million years, representing 222 different populations of more than 70 extinct horse species. According to one of these scientists, Dr Nikos Solounias, "Living horses are anything but typical examples of the dietary ecology of this once great group of mammals."
(*http://www.horsetalk.co.nz/news/2011/03/026.shtml*)

Additionally, researchers have now concluded that large mammals, including ancient horses, also altered their diets as their climate changed. Both of these new findings contradict a common assumption that species maintain a dietary niche. By studying the carbon and oxygen isotopes incorporated into mammalian tooth enamel, scientists are attempting to determine the diets of fossil horses.
(*http://www.horsetalk.co.nz/news/2009/06/056.shtml*)

One of the scientists leading this exciting investigation is Dr. Bruce MacFadden, the Curator of Vertebrate Palaeontology at the Florida Museum of Natural History. Author of the book, *Fossil Horses*, he is using a new scientific method to study ancient horse teeth for traces of how the animal lived millions of years ago. MacFadden believes horses ate a combination of foods.

"This study is noteworthy because it's the first to be published that looks at the combination of these two techniques to understand ancient diets and the ecology of a particular group of extinct mammals," he said.

Modern grazers such as horses and zebras develop elongated (high-crowned) teeth because they eat gritty, abrasive grasses, while browsers such as deer, whose diet consists mainly of soft leafy vegetation, have short teeth, MacFadden said. But MacFadden's research on six species of prehistoric horses that lived 5 million years ago shows that despite all the horses having elongated teeth, they were a combination of browsers, grazers and mixed feeders.

(http://www.flmnh.ufl.edu/sciencestories/2005/fossil_horses.htm
http://horsetalk.co.nz/archives/2007/12/166.shtml)

The new investigation technique, known as dental mesowear analysis, enables academics to reconstruct the diets of extinct species by measuring food-related wear and tear on fossil teeth.

In a related development, contrary to popular belief, grains recently found on 30,000-year-old grinding stones indicate prehistoric humans did not only rely on a meat-centred diet but also dined on an early form of bread.

(http://www.nytimes.com/2010/10/19/science/19bread.html)

Alternatively, should MacFadden and the other scientists be looking for traces of ancient protein, as well as vanished vegetation, on fossil equine teeth?

Hunter Humans Riding Hunter Horses

The modern equine mouth provides a clue to this intriguing possibility because, in addition to the flat herbivore teeth residing there, horses have canine and wolf teeth as well. Conical canine teeth are used on meat, not plant life. Oddly enough, these canine teeth are shared with humans, not carnivores.

Additionally, the jaw of a modern horse can move side to side, to chew vegetation, or front to back, for consuming meat. Once again, humans also have this adaptable mandible capacity.

Thus, like their human riders, horses possess teeth, jaws and digestive systems which would allow them to be omnivorous. Could these biological facts help explain why the ancient Greeks chose the centaur, a horse-human composite, to represent man's unity with the animal world?

(*http://forum.horsetopia.com/general-horse-advice/54666-carnivorous-horses-2.html*)

Likewise the Greeks believed that the centaurs, who were half-human and half-horse, were also hunters and meat-eaters.

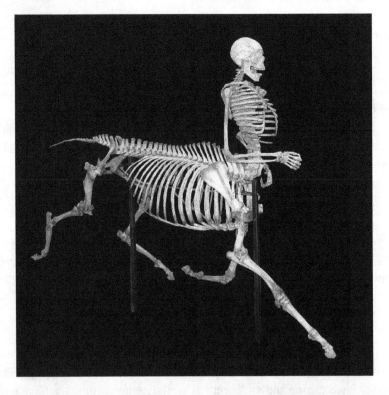

A centaur skeleton, constructed from zebra and human bones.

One of the earliest clues regarding these mythical beasts is dated to 1750 BC, at which time the Kassites used boundary stones, often incised with supernatural figures, to make and protect the perimeters of their lands in Babylonia. Some of these stones depicted beings that were half horse and half man, who probably functioned as guardian spirits. These early carnivorous centaurs were portrayed as hunters, carrying bows as weapons.

(*The Centaur – Its History and Meaning in Human Culture* by Dr. Elizabeth Atwood Lawrence, The Journal of Popular Culture, Volume 27, Issue 4, pages 57–68, Spring 1994.)

Scientists are still struggling to determine when humans first mounted the horse. Those events most likely occurred thousands of years ago, somewhere along what I have termed the Equestrian Equator, the ancient grasslands which once covered the earth from the plains of Hungary to the far edge of Mongolia.

While the search for evidence connected to the origins of riding continues, legends of the centaur, as well as newly discovered information regarding meat-eating horses, raise new possibilities.

With Kafka's story of how horses and humans shared meat as a background, we might wonder if early humans, horses and dogs all profited from a beneficial collective existence, one in which a combination of their individual skills resulted in a protein-rich diet that they shared round the campfire?

Recalling how Shackleton and Socks shared the Maujee Ration, one cannot help but speculate if the horse, with his evolved sense of herd loyalty, realized, like the dog before him, that there was a dietary advantage to be gained by cooperating with humans.

Exploring the Possibilities

French Long Rider Jean Louis Gouraud has reported that geneticists in his country have uncovered evidence indicating horses did not originate on the herbivore branch of the Tree of Life, but rather on that of the carnivores.

When contacted by the LRG-AF, Dr. Matthew Binns, a leading equine geneticist at Cambridge University, confirmed that "horses will share their genes with carnivorous and herbivorous mammals."

Additional thoughts on the biological possibility of meat-eating horses were discovered in an unlikely source, the computer laboratory at Cambridge University.

During an intensive study into "the exploration of possibilities," Colin Johnson documented how a potential occurrence or character can be placed within a hierarchy based upon historical, biological, physical and logical evidence. To illustrate his study, the computer expert used horses.

The notion of a flying horse, he concluded, is biologically impossible due to constraints of energy expenditure, bone strength, etcetera. Yet the Cambridge scholar went on to conclude that, "A carnivorous horse, however, is biologically possible; it is just not historically possible, as horse populations never found themselves in a situation where meat-eating was necessary or advantageous."

(Search and notions of creativity – PHD by Colin G. Johnson, Computing Laboratory, University of Kent at Canterbury)

Evidence indicates that we are dealing with a multi-faceted equine. It can choose to be a flight animal. Like man, it can kill. It can choose to be herbivorous. Like man, it can eat meat.

This begs the question: if the horse is separated from the cow, camel and sheep on the Tree of Life, then did the horse have meat-eating roots? Was the four-toed Dawn Horse an omnivore who evolved into the one-toed herbivore we recognize today? Or are there, as Hamlet warned, "more things in heaven and earth than are dreamt of in your philosophy"?

The answer might be found under water.

Meat-Eating Water Horses

Ancient Greeks named the hippopotamus "horse of the river," even though it's not actually related to the land-based equine. While the reasoning behind that linguistic decision is shrouded in mystery, what isn't under debate is the hippo's bad temper. It is one of the most dangerous creatures in Africa.

Yet even though its aggression was well documented, until recently it was believed to be an herbivorous mammal. New evidence has derailed that idea.

In the late 1980s, the infamous drug baron, Pablo Escobar imported four hippos to jazz up the private menagerie he kept at his hideout in Columbia. After the outlaw's death, the ownerless "river horses" did what free hippos like to do. They had sex, multiplied, began roaming along the local river and started attacking humans and cattle.
(*http://en.wikipedia.org/wiki/Hippopotamus*)

Soon afterwards, a field biologist in Zimbabwe provided an eyewitness account describing hippos killing and devouring impalas. "It seems almost incredible," wrote Dr. Joseph Dudley, "that carnivorous feeding behaviour by hippos, even if of very infrequent occurrence, could have gone unreported for so long."
(*http://search.sabinet.co.za/WebZ/images/ejour/wild/wild_v28_n2_a4.p df?sessionid=0&format=F*)

More recently a group of foreign teachers visiting Africa were surprised while walking. A large hippo emerged from the jungle in front of them, crossed the road where they were standing, walked straight up to a large calf who was tethered nearby, and began eating the animal alive. The teachers, who were too terrified to move, stood frozen in place while the carnage went on, after which the hippo returned to the jungle and the tourists fled.
(*http://laelaps.wordpress.com/2007/08/07/carnivorous-hippos/*)

Why do meat-eating hippos matter to the LRG-AF investigation?
Because the local African guide informed the foreign teachers that though they were shocked at witnessing a meat-eating hippo, he wasn't. In fact, he reported, local natives had long been aware of such events and recognized the behaviour of the cow-crunching hippo as not being out of character.

Unlike the modern horse world, the Africans understood the true nature of the "river horse."

Then what factors could be contributing to such a fundamental modern misinterpretation of the horse's diet and emotional behaviour?

Though originally believed to be a herbivore, eyewitness accounts have confirmed that, like horses, hippopotami kill other animals and eat them. This image shows a hippo biting a wildebeest as it attempts to swim the Masai Mara river in Kenya.

Mistaken Messages

If humanity is to build on what it knows, instead of what it thinks, then we must begin by realizing that that persistent error exists in today's equestrian community.

An example of this began in 1904. That was the year Kaiser Wilhelm made the first political recording, American engineers began work on the Panama Canal, and the explorer, Henry Morton Stanley died. It was also the year that eohippus was first described as "being the size of a Fox Terrier."

How did an English dog become linked to a 55 million year-old horse?

This description was originally issued in 1904 when Henry Fairfield Osborne published this description in an article entitled, *The Evolution of the Horse in America.*

"We may imagine the earliest herds of horses in the lower Eocene as resembling a lot of Fox-Terriers in size," Osborne wrote. For more than a hundred years, this description was thereafter faithfully copied and re-copied by lazy researchers who never actually bothered to find out what size the ancient horse actually was.

(*http://stevyncolgan.blogspot.com/2008_01_01_archive.html*)

More recently, Professor Richard Bulliet has warned of the emergence of a serious new problem connected to understanding horses accurately. Bulliet is a professor of history at Columbia University, one of whose specialities is the influence of animals in the development of human society. In his provocative look at human-animal relations, Bulliet argues that we live in an era of "post-domesticity" in which people live far away, "both physically and psychologically," from the animals whose food and hides they rely on.
(*http://www.columbia.edu/~rwb3/*)

Bulliet contends that in our current era civilized man has undergone a sea-change in terms of his relationship with animals. People remain dependent upon animal products, even though they no longer have any daily involvement with actual producing animals. Because they lack the elemental interspecies dynamic enjoyed by their ancestors, basic knowledge of animal actions has been replaced by a quaint, and ultimately destructive, apologia for aggression displayed either for or against animals. The result, Bulliet cautions is, "a pronounced humanization of companion animals that shows up particularly in their becoming characters in novels, movies, and cartoons."
(*http://www.lrgaf.org/voa/bulliet.htm*
Hunters, Herders and Hamburgers, Richard Bulliet, Columbia University Press, 2007)

Thus, the average human being's daily knowledge of equine nature has diminished to an alarming extent. It has been replaced by a Disney-esque version of events where there is no dark side to nature. This is particularly true in Anglophone countries, where the appearance of books and films now commonly depicts horses in romantic terms such as Angel Horses: Divine Messengers of Hope.
(*Angel Horses: Divine Messengers of Hope*, Allen Anderson, Linda Anderson, New World Library, 2006)

Historical, literary, scientific, emotional, biological, digestive and dental evidence provided so far prove the existence of this Anomaly. Yet equine behaviour which is deemed aberrant or abnormal from this new social message has been largely hidden, erased or ignored.

If meat-eating hippos are socially acceptable, why has modern man given his loyalty to an equestrian misconception which denies the existence of murderous and meat-eating horses?

There is a variety of factors involved, including money, media, medicine and manipulation of the facts.

Equestrian Amnesia

To begin with, we must not lose sight of the fact that until the end of the 19th century a large percentage of humanity knew that horses were capable of eating meat and behaving in an aggressive manner.

In 1908 *Bailey's Cyclopedia of American Agriculture* reported that horses could eat meat, though they did not require it. Further south in Chile, Dr. Philippi, that country's best-known zoologist, reported cases of meat-eating equines in that region too.

When did we begin to forget such vital lessons from our horse history? What slew our collective mounted memories without a trace of regret? How did mankind's equestrian amnesia become so advanced that 6,000 years of wisdom managed to be lost in two generations?

Part of the blame is connected to rise of the automobile culture, as the motorized age undermined the need for horses in transportation, agriculture and warfare. The resulting equinocide saw millions of horses destroyed, as mankind eagerly embraced the motor and destroyed the horses which had served him for millennia. If, for example, the American horse population had continued to grow at its normal rate, by 1930 there would have been an estimated 6.5 million horses living and working in the cities alone. Instead there were only 1.5 million, and their numbers would soon be radically reduced even further.

(*www.lrgaf.org/slaughter/savin.htm*
The Horse in the City by Clay McShane and Joel Tarr, John Hopkins University Press in 2007)

Thus, because of the overall demise of horses in farming, military and travel, the groundwork was laid for an intellectual equestrian vacuum. As fewer humans needed horses, reduced numbers retained any collective experience or personal knowledge of them. The result was a viral spread of urban values which wiped away centuries of equestrian knowledge.

Adding to this collective human amnesia is the contributing fact that the vast majority of people who are still involved with horses primarily limit their dealings to mares and geldings.

An example of this was demonstrated by Professor Bulliet. He points out that in a post-domestic world 98% of the horse-owning population never sees a stallion, except perhaps on a race-track.

Thanks to a motorized existence and an industrialized monoculture, millions of people have become largely out of touch with the natural world of horses. The result is that first-hand knowledge regarding dangerous equine behaviour has been replaced with a fairytale view of horses which portrays them as helpless, grass-eating victims.

Because of massive equestrian amnesia, modern man has forgotten how dangerous equines can be. (Photo: www.mmoabc.com)

Medical Misdiagnosis

Nor does the modern veterinarian community seem to have recalled these historical lessons either.

What must be appreciated is how relatively young equine medicine is.

The American census of 1850 recorded only forty-six individuals who practised equine medicine. At that time the majority of horse owners relied on quack cures or remedies based upon folklore. That changed in 1872, when the worst equestrian epidemic in history, known as the "great epizootic," crippled the North American continent.

Imagine an equestrian health disaster that crippled all of America, halted the government in Washington DC, stopped the ships in New York, burned Boston to the ground and forced the cavalry to fight the Apaches on foot. It was an equine tragedy so deadly that one wave of the infection swept south like a Biblical plague from its origin in Toronto, Canada, down the Atlantic Seaboard to Havana, Cuba, leaving everything in its path in ruins in weeks, while another branch simultaneously raced west to the Pacific.

Over the course of one year, September 1872 - September 1873, equine influenza engulfed the equine population of Canada and its maritime provinces, the United States and its western territories, Mexico, Central America and the Caribbean islands. Virtually every horse, mule and donkey, particularly in urban areas of the Americas, was sickened and temporarily disabled.

Unluckily, the United States was effectively bereft of any veterinary medical education when the epizootic struck that nation.

Consequently, the massive equestrian epidemic which devastated the American equestrian population prompted a national desire to promote equestrian health studies. Thanks to the newly created animal science programmes the 1890 census reported more than 6,500 licensed veterinarians.
(*www.lrgaf.org/medical/epizootic.htm*)

What should be taken in to account is that there was a brief window of history, from approximately 1880 until 1925, whereby there were veterinarians who may have had eye-witness experience or first hand knowledge of meat-eating and murderous equines. For example, Professor Gleason tamed the man-killing stallion, Rysdyk, before thousands of people in New York City.

Thereafter, as the influence of the automobile grew, and the horse was reduced to the role of domestic pet, this wisdom largely passed out of existence even within the equine medical community, the result being that 21st century contemporary veterinarians appear to have for-gotten the existence of the O'Reilly Anomaly.

This was demonstrated by the publication in 2002 of the original magazine article wherein an American veterinarian, Dr. Sue Mc-Donnell, was asked by the editors to explain to readers how horse pets could consume other animals – and she could not provide that answer. (*Carnivorous Horses* by Dr. Sue McDonnell, The Horse – October, 2002, page 61.)

In a follow-up article published several years later, Dr. McDonnell, recalled how she had originally been mystified when confronted by international evidence suggesting the unsuspected existence of carnivorous horses.

"While taking questions from the audience at a one-day behaviour program in New Zealand, a well-respected horse owner and trainer des-cribed behaviour she had recently witnessed in a horse involving a scenario I had never heard of or thought about. None of the 200 or so horse owners in the audience had either. Then within a month, *The Horse* magazine received two emails about the same peculiar behaviour. Again, none of the staff there had heard of such behaviour in horses, and they referred the questions to me. At a recent inter-national meeting of horse behaviourists, I asked around about this behaviour. While most people had heard or seen certain aspects of the behaviour, no one had experience or knowledge from literature of the more disturbing elements," Dr. McDonnell wrote.

Since then other medical authorities have reinforced a similar view of the horse's peaceful nature and vegetarian diet.

"Wild horses are herbivorous prey animals," wrote Dr. Victoria Aspinall, a Member of Great Britain's Royal College of Veterinary Surgeons. (*The Complete Textbook of Veterinary Nursing* by Dr. Victoria Aspinall, Butterworth Heinemann, 2006)

"Horses are a prey species; we humans are predators," likewise reported Sarah Probst, an Information Specialist at the University of Illinois College of Veterinary Medicine. (*http://www.arabianknightsfarms.com/akf/vetinfo/vet02.htm*)

Whereas this is largely true, historical evidence indicates that this is not the complete or accurate story. The result is that a vast majority of today's equestrian medical research is aimed at genetic research and sports medicine.

Meanwhile, previous medical knowledge connected to this Anomaly dwindled and then disappeared in a fog of cultural neglect.

Academic Apathy

In 1918 there were an estimated 21,550,000 horses, ponies and mules labouring in the United States alone. They worked on farms, toiled in cities and maintained contact with the remote parts of the country. By 1930 less than a third of these animals remained.

Mankind lost more than the horse when he replaced the equine with the automobile. Various types of equestrian knowledge, gathered and perfected over five thousand years, died without a whisper between the dawning of the Model T and the advent of the black and white television.

Today there is a surprising lack of intellectual curiosity about our collective equestrian past. For the past few decades scientists have wrongly viewed the horse as a nostalgic relic of a pre-industrial age. While there have been recent significant breakthroughs in genetic research, the academic community has played a part in allowing the world's equestrian heritage to atrophy to the point of intellectual extinction.

In a world dying from inadequate equestrian investigation, a growing number of universities are offering what are known as "Mickey Mouse" degrees which are of dubious academic merit. For example, one hundred British universities spend more than £40 million a year on courses such as "fashion buying" and "pirateology." Plus, while a student can study the archaeology of sports, food, music and rocks, no university offers a degree in equine-based archaeology. Nor are other areas of interest in the equestrian scientific arena being adequately developed. The result is that, with the exception of issues related to equine health, there is a deficit of international equestrian academic leadership.

A Censored Media

You might be tempted to think that a story about murderous or meat-eating horses would sell a few magazines. You'd be wrong. Editors won't touch it.

Thankfully, in 1954 National Geographic magazine didn't censor the news detailing how the Kazakh tribe had fled on meat-eating horses. Apparently those editors saw the words but didn't react to the discovery.

In sharp contrast was the more recent indifference displayed by the editors of Scientific American magazine. Though presented with an opportunity to examine all of the accumulated evidence found within this book, that publication declined to investigate it.

(*Letter from the LRG-AF to John Rennie, Editor, Scientific American, dated December 10, 2007*)

Nor is the equestrian press leading the battle to understand atypical equine behaviour.

A recent informal survey revealed that 76% of the horse owners surveyed no longer purchased monthly equestrian magazines.

Why?

Speaking off the record to the LRG-AF, an equestrian editor said, "The trouble with horse magazines is instead of giving readers something that would shock, educate or change their perceptions, they are too set on the results of focus groups, readership demographic surveys and chasing the market share. They give the readers what they think they want, repackaged kitsch aimed at the lowest common denominator of reader (and rider)."

(*Email to LRG-AF dated March 22, 2008*)

In the corporate-dominated magazine world, where finances always come first, meaningful research is passed over in preference to ads for expensive horse equipment and colourful riding togs. The result is that for the last fifty years, though the public yearned for something meaningful, there has been little cross-community discussion undertaken between academics and mainstream equestrian magazine editors.

Moreover, recent magazine coverage indicates that news connected to meat-eating and murderous horses was erased or curtailed. What did the censors not want the public to see?

Ironically, one of the most notorious cases of modern equine abuse contains an ancient clue which was effectively buried by this indifferent arm of the media.

Shakespeare's cannibal horses spring to mind when connected to a recent English example of carnivorous equine behaviour. This occurred in January, 2008, when British authorities converged on a property in Buckinghamshire.

What they discovered was a "horror farm" that shocked the world. Dead horses had been incinerated in an outdoor pit. Weak animals had been hit by a Land Rover and left to expire. More than 30 horses were found lying dead on the ground. Nearly a hundred were standing in giant heaps of manure, starving to death. These details were widely released.

Yet only one news source appears to have reported that a local animal control officer was quoted as saying that he believed the surviving horses had lived by resorting to eating their dead comrades.

One of the animal officials called in to the scene said: "It is quite apparent that these animals have been without food a long time." He said they thought that the horses had survived by eating the bodies of the dead animals.
(*www.environmentalgraffiti.com/ecology/31-horses-dead-of-neglect/68 www.horsetalk.co.nz/news/2008/01/040.shtml*)

This might just be deemed squeamish reporting, if evidence did not also indicate that the majority of the equestrian magazines have a strong financial incentive not to question the role of the horse as a passive victim of human aggression.

A Million Dollar Myth

Science is mankind's one truly global culture, whose common vision transcends all differences of nationality and faith. However, as equestrian wisdom has declined, ignorance and superstition increased. The result is that we are witnessing the rise of an age of equestrian disinformation, one where a trusting public can graze on nonsense packaged to look like fact.

The worst danger is the increase of hocus-pocus horsemanship. These people, who peddle various equestrian superstitions over the internet and in expensive clinics, urge a departure from rational thought and embrace emotionalism instead. The cumulative effect is the emergence of a 21st century horse world which is in danger of being overwhelmed by equestrian superstition and is infected by various equine personality cults, all of which threaten to undermine the intellectual integrity of serious equestrian science.

(*www.lrgaf.org/voa/authority.htm*)

In a related development, psychologists have warned the public about "normalisation," i.e. the more we are told something, the more likely we are to believe it is true.

An excellent example of this concept can be found within the multimillion dollar horse-whispering industry, which encourages the mistaken assumption that the horse is consistently a timid grass-eater who is terrified of predatory humans.

One of the most well known proponents of this belief is the celebrated American author, trainer and lecturer, Monty Roberts, who said, "The horse is a prey animal."

(*www.montyroberts.com/ju_ask_monty_1204.html*)

"Horses are a prey species and we humans are predators," repeats a clone.

"The horse is naturally fearful," sings one more.

"Everyone knows that horses are flight animals," cries the chorus.

This misconception is being continually strengthened by a host of other sympathetic outlets.

"Prey animal psychology is all about understanding the horse is a prey animal whose first instinct is to flee/retreat/move the feet when afraid," lectured "natural horse" trainer, Sylvia Scott.

(*www.naturalhorsetraining.com/trainingtips59.html*)

The concept has moved from the round pen to the internet, thanks to journalists like David MacMahon, who writes, "A horse is a prey ani-

mal and as a prey animal, they are always looking for an escape from threatening situations."
(*http://ezinearticles.com/?Is-There-a-Surefire-Way-to-Prevent-Horse-Bucking?&id=3885613*)

From articles the concept became enshrined in books, such as *Horses for Dummies*, where we find horses described as "a prey species."
(*www.facebook.com/pages/HORSES-FOR-DUMMIES/193162431683*)

In August, 2010 British television star, Martin Clunes, reinforced this notion on the programme *Horsepower*, when he asked Monty Roberts to explain "how humans managed to tame such a huge, fearful prey animal?"
(*www.yourhorse.co.uk/Your-Horse-News/Search-Results/General-news/August-10/18-Aug-Martin-Clunes-meets-Monty-Roberts-in-ITV-documentary-/*)

Why pretend that horses are victims to be pitied?
Lack of education is one reason. Financial gain is another.
According to one source, a private clinic was held by one of the world's leading horse whisperers. Twelve people attended, each of whom had paid $40,000 for the weekend lecture.
(*Telephone conversation with the LRG-AF on October, 28, 2007*)

Horse-whispering clinics, books, lectures, and an assortment of products have all resulted in the propagation of a multi-million dollar industry, despite the fact that history demonstrates instead that the horse is in fact capable of murderous violence, and that if presented with a certain set of circumstances, these "prey" animals will become anthropophagic and definitely eat meat, survive on meat and, if necessary, kill and consume other animals, equines and humans.

The documentation of this behaviour contradicts the current popular image of man the predator preying on the horse, his helpless victim.

Despite nearly four thousand years of evidence indicating how horses have been the cause of violent human death and specie wide destruction, modern horse whisperers perpetuate the myth that the horse is a timid "prey" animal who needs protection from mankind and carnivores (Photo: www.mmoabc.com)

Conflicting Evidence

Once we acknowledge the existence of these anomalous horses, we realize that additional evidence of its existence is in plain sight. Thus, while horse whisperers continued to label equines as passive prey animals, astounding conflicting evidence was freely available to the public.

One notable example was revealed in 2002 when a series of graphic photographs were recorded in New Mexico and then released around the world via the internet. The images show Jody Anglin's mule, Barry, savaging a dead mountain lion. In an interview with reporter Steven

Richards, Anglin, who has been hunting mountain lions for years, explained how his mule developed an intense hatred for the big cats.

"I have talked to Jody a couple of times," the reporter, Richards, wrote for *Western Mule* magazine, "trying to be sure to get the story correct. Jody is 25 and hunts lions as often as he can. Jody was telling me when he first started hunting he would take his hounds and walk to areas that had lions. Then he got Barry the mule and that made hunting easier."

(*www.westernmulemagazine.com*)

"Jody has had Berry since 1998 and he is an 11 year old mule now. When Jody first got the mule, and after Jody shot the first lion out, Berry casually came over to the lion and just nuzzled the lion and casually nibbled it. With each lion Berry just got more aggressive. Jody said it didn't take more than two lions and Berry got really aggressive to the lion until he got to braying real loud and couldn't wait to get the cat."

(*www.westernmulemagazine.com/image/webimage/MULE%20VS%20 MOUNTAIN%20LION2.pdf*)

The manner in which Barry the mule grabbed the puma, violently shook it, then pinned it under his front legs mirrors the tactics used 146 years earlier when the quagga pinned and killed the hyena. Yet rather than having prompted an overdue debate, this evidence was ignored.

What occurred instead was that modern man's misunderstanding of horses inspired unforeseen consequences among the young. British equestrian experts, it was learned, were encouraging students to alter their diet in a vain attempt not to frighten their horses.

"I am currently studying the first of four BHS [British Horse Society] horse care courses at equine college. I was amazed to discover that your horse can tell if you are a meat eater, in which case you would be a predator to him. It is recommended that you do not go near your horse straight after eating a meaty meal. This has really got me thinking of becoming a vegetarian. Have you turned vegetarian over this? Or were you already a veggie when you bought your horse? I'd love to know your thoughts on this subject?"

(*http://uk.answers.yahoo.com/question/index?qid=20101114105335AA BpflO*)

Barry the mule first savages a mountain lion previously slain by the rider. Then he tosses aside the dead predator with contempt.

The discovery that impressionable young riders are being encouraged to avoid eating meat ignores the conflicting evidence connected to the multi-faceted nature of the horse.

Regardless of this academic misdirection, a growing number of everyday horse owners have voiced serious doubts about this newly minted mythology.

A Simmering Suspicion

Maintaining loyalty to an outdated equestrian concept is nothing new. In 1847 the renowned historian, Rollo Springfield, warned that the equestrian community was in danger of becoming rooted in tradition. The result, he said, would be an obstinate refusal to examine new ideas.

"These men will continue from generation to generation doing something absurd from force of habit and utter want of thought," Springfield advised.

Despite a lack of official answers, horse owners world wide have become increasingly eager to discuss mysterious behaviour which they cannot otherwise explain. One such equestrian chat room presents multiple answers to the question posed by a bewildered woman named Sherry.

She wrote to ask, "Ok, this may seem like the strangest question you will ever read, but I just have to know. Who has a horse that eats meat? My friend has one and so do I."

While Sherry's mount preferred hamburgers, other readers quickly wrote to describe how their horses were eagerly eating meat sandwiches, turkey, salami, sausages and hotdogs. (*www.horsegroomingsupplies.com/horse-forums/meat-eating-horses-54951.html*)

Another popular equine website has a chat room which offers further evidence of a wide equestrian diet. This one includes roast beef, ham and Kentucky Fried Chicken, (*http://forum.horsetopia.com/general-horse-advice/54666-carnivorous-horses.html*)

In late nineteenth century France, Professor Rouhet taught his stallion, Germinal, to enjoy a sophisticated meal with him

Some riders have already come to the conclusion that today's belief in harmless horses is mistaken.

"Most horses will gladly eat cooked meat and I knew one that would run down, kill and eat rabbits," writes Kathleen.

(*www.cookingjunkies.com/rec-food-cooking/new-study-shows-deer-eat-meat-28668.html*)

Regardless of these eyewitness accounts, many people prefer wilful blindness rather than admit the existence of these horses.

"Horses resort to cannibalism? Horses will never eat each other. I can't believe what I'm reading," reported one disgruntled chat room reader.

It is no wonder this person was confused, as there were plenty of "experts" busy reinforcing the wrong idea.

All Experts is an internet website devoted to "answering your questions."

Dorothy Morris-Robinson is one such specialist. A dedicated horse-woman with a background in dressage, cross country obstacles and show jumping, she is quoted on All Experts as saying, "No matter what equestrian discipline you prefer, the result must be beauty in motion."

One internet reader posed this intelligent question to Ms. Morris-Robinson.

"Why don't horses need meat to survive unlike humans?"

Morris-Robinson responded, "Horses don't eat meat because they are strict herbivores. That means that their digestive system is not able to digest meat. If a horse ate meat he would probably get sick."
(*http://en.allexperts.com/q/Horses-702/don-t-horses-eat.htm*)

As Professor Bulliet points out, modern humans tend to harbour an idealistic mental image of the horse as being a spiritually pure and innocent creature, akin to the unicorn. The notion of horses devouring meat or killing other animals shatters this idealized image.

Lost Lessons

Ironically, though the mainstream horse world continues to overlook multiple sources of evidence, ancient cultures and modern scholars have jointly confirmed that the horse isn't a frightened victim. That proof was found on the grassy steppes of the Equestrian Equator, a vast corridor of steppe land which runs from Mongolia to Hungary.

Professor Jack Weatherford is one of the world's leading experts on the Mongol empire. In his thought-provoking book, *Genghis Khan and the Making of the Modern World*, Weatherford described how, thanks to the horse, the legendary tribal chieftain created the largest empire in history and organized the first universal postal system.

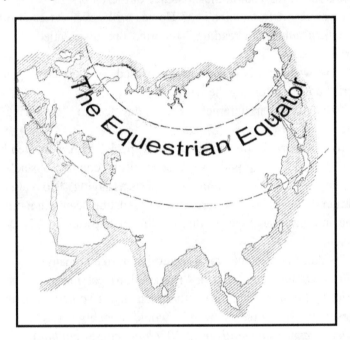

The Equestrian Equator is a term the author coined to describe the ancient grasslands which once covered the earth from the plains of Hungary to the far edge of Mongolia.

Weatherford's latest work, *The Secret History of the Mongol Queens*, explained how before his death Genghis Khan made it possible for his daughters and female descendants to wield the largest amount of political power in history. Like their famous forefather, these mounted Mongol queens led their warriors into battle, with one queen, Mandhuhai, even charging into battle while pregnant.
(*http://en.wikipedia.org/wiki/Jack_Weatherford*)

Though courage and leadership were vitally important to the Mongols, their military success was based upon the critical fact that they controlled the largest horse herds in the history of mankind. Legend has it that Genghis Khan alone maintained a special herd of 10,000 snow-white horses.

In addition to studying rare documents written in archaic languages, Weatherford also made extensive equestrian journeys throughout Mongolia. While undertaking what he called the 'archaeology of move-ment,' these long rides gave the American professor a unique scholastic insight into Mongolian equestrian history. What he points out in his books is that the Mongols comprehend the true nature of the horse, in a way similar to how Africans understand the hippopotamus.

During his research, Weatherford documented equestrian behaviour which flies in the face of the myth of the passive horse. To explain how that came about, we must first dispense with the old legend that horses fear wolves. Mongols, the professor learned, knew that aggressive horses were fully capable of putting wolves to flight.

"The wolf pack cannot threaten the strong stallion, who can attack with his hooves and severely injure or kill an adult wolf.....From thousands of years together on the steppe, the two animals know each other's threats and each other's defences."

And Weatherford isn't wrong, as other documents provide more striking examples of horses routing this legendary predator.

In the rare book, entitled *Anecdotes of the Habits and Instinct of Animals,* published in London in 1852, the author R. Lee recounts an eyewitness account describing massive herds of wild horses on the Russian steppes, then provides this evidence of aggressive equine behaviour.

"In the spring come the wolves, being very fond of young foals; so they constantly prowl round the herds, never attacking them by day if they are numerous; but come at night, and if they are scattered, they make a rush upon their victims. The stallions, however, charge at them; and they take flight only, however, to return and secure a straggling foal, to whose rescue the mother comes, and herself perishes. When this is found out, a terrible battle ensues; the foals are placed in the centre, the mares encircle them, charging the wolves in front; tearing them with their teeth, and trampling them with their fore-feet, always using the latter, and not the hind feet; the stallions rush about, and often kill a wolf with one blow; they then pick up the body with their teeth, and throw it to the mares, who trample upon it till its original form is utterly destroyed. If eight or ten hungry wolves should pull down a stallion, the whole herd will revenge him, and almost always destroy the wolves; who, however, generally try to avoid these great battles, and chase a mare or foal separated from the rest, creep up to them, imitating a watchdog, and wagging their tails, spring at the throat of the mare; and then the foal is carried off. Even this will not always succeed, and if the mare gives alarm, the wolf is pursued by herd and keeper, and his only chance of escape is to throw himself head-foremost down the steep sides of a ravine.

(*www.gutenberg.org/ebooks/21973*)

Wild horse herds living on the steppes were capable of defending their young and killing the wolves which threatened the herd's safety.

Nor was this the first such account, as in 1847 British author, Rollo Springfield, left this detailed record of a herd of wild horses also putting a wolf pack to flight.

"The spring, though in so many respects a season of enjoyment, is not without its drawbacks. The wolves, also, have to indemnify themselves for the severe fast of the winter, and are just as desirous as the horses to get themselves into good condition again. The foals, too, are just then most delicate, and a wolf will any day prefer a young foal to a sheep or a calf. The wolf accordingly is constantly prowling about the herd during the spring, and the horses are bound to be always prepared to do battle in defence of the younger members of the community. The wolf, as the weaker party, trusts more to cunning than strength. For a party of wolves openly to attack a herd at noon-day, would be to rush upon certain destruction; and, however severely the wolf may be pressed by hunger, he knows his own weakness too well, to venture on so absurd an act of temerity.

At night, indeed, if the herd happened to be a little scattered, and the wolves in tolerable numbers, they will sometimes attempt to rush, and a general battle ensues. An admirable spirit of coalition then displays itself among the horses. On the first alarm, stallions and mares come charging up to the threatened point, and attack the wolves with an impetuosity, that often puts the prowlers to instant flight. Soon, however, if they feel themselves sufficiently numerous, they return and hover about the herd, till some poor foal straggles a few yards from the main body, when it is seized by the enemy, while the mother, springing to its rescue, is nearly certain to share the same fate.

Then it is that the battle begins in real earnest.

The mares form a circle, within which the foals take shelter. We have seen pictures in which the horses are represented in a circle, presenting their hind hooves to the wolves, who thus appear to have the free choice to fight, or to let it alone. Such pictures are the mere result of imagination, and bear very little resemblance to the reality; for the wolf has, in general, to pay much more dearly for his partiality to horseflesh. The horses, when they attack wolves, do not turn their tails towards them, but charge upon them in a solid phalanx, tearing them with their teeth, and trampling on them with their feet.

The stallions do not fall into the phalanx, but gallop about with streaming tails, and flying manes, and seem to act at once as generals, trumpeteers, and standard-bearers. When they see a wolf, they rush upon him with reckless fury, mouth to mouth, or if they use their feet as weapons of defence, it is always with the front, and not the hinder hoof, that the attack is made. With one blow the stallion often kills his enemy, or stuns him. If so, he snatches the body up with his teeth and flings it to the mares, who trample upon it till it becomes hard to say what kind of animal the skin belonged to."

(*The Horse and his Rider* by Rollo Springfield, Chapman & Hall, London, 1847)

With the wolf stories in mind, we must ask ourselves why we should care if stallions once snatched their enemies with sharp teeth, shook them to pieces and then killed them without mercy? Why do folktales about horses defending their young against predators matter? What happens when modern man misjudges the horse?

As current news stories confirm, when these lessons are lost, human beings die.

Lisette and Rysdyk aren't demons from another age. Their deadly descendants are among us still.

Deadly Horses

Though he is better known today for having created Sherlock Holmes, Sir Arthur Conan Doyle was a devoted student of history and a keen observer of deadly horses. In his book, *Sir Nigel*, Conan Doyle not only provided a lengthy account of the Hundred Years War, he described the actions of a stallion who had slain many men.

These events occurred when a number of hapless 14th century priests attempted to capture the stallion. The resulting attack on the churchmen was merciless.

"The great creature turned upon his would-be captors and with flashing teeth grabbed the prior and began shaking him as a dog does a rat... A loud wail of horror arose from the priests, as the savage horse, the most terrible and cruel in its anger of all creatures on earth, bit and shook and trampled the withering body."

(*Sir Nigel* by Sir Arthur Conan Doyle, McClure, Phillips & Co., New York, 1906.)

The method by which this fictional English stallion slew the priest matches the eyewitness descriptions of the real Russian stallion killing a wolf. The infuriated horse catches the victim in his teeth, shakes him viciously, throws him into the air and then stomps him to death.

Why would a scene on the Russian steppe nearly two hundred years ago matter to modern horse owners? Because the evidence of how angry stallions react when their foals are threatened has not disappeared.

In December of 2007 a scene matching that written by Conan Doyle occurred in Australia. Only this time it wasn't fiction. A toddler died in hospital from "spinal injuries sustained when a stallion picked him up and threw him into the air."

According to news accounts, Matthew Petricevich was 18 months old when he went under a fence and approached the horses. The result was that the stallion killed the child before his nearby mother could intervene.

(*http://horsetalk.co.nz/archives/2007/12/093.shtml*)

Why would this previously pleasant horse, which had been a trusted member of the family for years, react like this? Because the child had been trying to reach the foals which the stallion was protecting. Why was the child killed? Because the horse was following his nature. The result was that the infant was slain and the grief-stricken parents destroyed the stallion which they had owned for eighteen years.

At first glance, one might be tempted instantly to define the actions of the Australian stallion as murder, which in turn would mean that Bucephalus, Lisette, the Dappled Demon and Rysdyk were monsters.

Yet new evidence indicates that the death of the child might be misinterpreted. What if throughout history mankind had not been witnessing cases of gleeful equine murder? What if new research indicated that some horses may have been acting in self-defence?

Species Chauvinism

Before we can investigate that possibility, we must first acknowledge the species chauvinism which mankind has long harboured. This
philosophy of superiority was famously articulated by René Descartes.
The 17th century Frenchman is often referred to as the "father of philosophy," but has never been described as a friend to the horse, for it was
Descartes who stated, "The reason animals do not speak as we do is not
that they lack the organs but that they have no thoughts."

Descartes taught that animals have no soul; therefore they can feel
no pain. A lack of pain and no soul, Descartes believed, meant that
animals could not reason. The result of this theology was that for
centuries many humans believed horses were mute, insensitive brutes,
provided by a generous God to be used like disposable machines. The
logical conclusion of Descartes philosophy was that though horses were
financially valuable, they were spiritually inferior.

This viewpoint was alive and well in 1910 when Lawrence Oates
was appointed to be in charge of Captain Robert Scott's horses in Antarctica. Oates, himself a British cavalry officer, famously said, "the
horse has no reasoning power."

Luckily, there were notable exceptions. For example, Historical
Long Rider Charles Darwin argued that the difference between humans
and animals was a matter of degree.

That debate continues.

Meanwhile, what is now generally accepted is that humans learn
from observation, while animals learn from first-hand experience. It is
also generally believed that animals experience fear, happiness and
boredom.

But do they understand revenge? Do they seek freedom? Do they
have a sense of right and wrong?

Horses and humans share an emotional similarity. They both have
the capability of hating their oppressors. But the majority of the time a
horse's sense of personal fear overcomes this hatred. Like humans, in
most cases a horse's sense of self-preservation overrides his self-
respect. He knows he is being tormented but he lacks the courage to
resist. It is the actions of this timid majority which have enforced the
mythology of the passive horse.

Yet startling new research indicates that there are exceptions. Like the handful of human prisoners who relentlessly plot an escape from prison, when some animals realize they are being unjustly treated they too are capable of attacking their tormentors and fleeing.

Animal Resistance

According to traditional belief, only humans possess emotions, culture, intellect, and the ability to resist. Dr. Jason Hribal is a historian who disagrees.

In his recently published book, *Fear of the Animal Planet: The Hidden History of Animal Resistance,* Hribal has documented how animals in captivity have deliberately resisted and rebelled against their captors in circuses, zoos, aquariums and research laboratories. He believes they are fighting for their liberty.

"The resistance," he writes, "became ever more evident. Captive animals escaped their cages. They attacked their keepers. They demanded more food. They refused to perform. They refused to reproduce. The resistance itself could be organized. Indeed, not only did the animals have a history, they were making history. For their resistance led directly to historical change."

Imprisoned animals, Hribal argues, are not making random decisions. One such example was provided by the actions of incarcerated elephants.

"These animals have the capability of inflicting large-scale fatalities. They are big, strong, and fast. Yet, when given the opportunity to plough through a crowd of visitors or stomp a row of spectators, they almost never do. Instead, they target specific individuals," he writes.

One notable example was provided when a circus elephant trampled the sadistic trainer who had repeatedly fed her lighted cigarettes.

"These animals understand that there will be consequences for incorrect actions. If they refuse to perform, if they attack a trainer, or if they escape their cage, they know that they will be beaten, have their food rations reduced, and be placed in solitary confinement. Captive animals know all of this and yet they still carry out such actions—often with a profound sense of determination. This is why these behaviours can be understood as a true form of resistance," Hribal wrote.

www.lrgaf.org

(Fear of the Animal Planet: The Hidden History of Animal Resistance,
Jason Hribal, AK Press, 2011
www.counterpunch.org/hribal02252010.html)

Though Hribal may have been the first to go into print with a book-length study regarding animal defiance, further evidence is available in the daily press.

For example, captive dolphins, like horses, are known to strike back at their tormentors. A billion dollar business has been developed to cater to the humans who eagerly pay $100 to swim alongside and stroke dolphins for a few minutes. Captured dolphins fetch up to $200,000 a piece and just one of these animals can earn a dolphinarium up to a million dollars a year in ticket sales. But there are drawbacks. When these highly intelligent animals are confined in small spaces, they have been known to attack tourists and slap visitors with their tails.

(Blood in the Water by Lauren St. John, The Sunday Times, March 20, 2011, page 8.)

Yet a dolphin's tail slap compares lightly with the rage of Tilikum the killer whale. Captured at the age of two, he is the largest Orca whale in confinement, a six-ton prisoner whose life and movements have been restricted to a puddle for the past twenty-eight years. Repeatedly bred and forced to entertain audiences, Tilikum has killed three people since 1991. In spite of this, his owners at Seaworld have no plans to retire Tilikum.

(http://en.wikipedia.org/wiki/Tilikum_(orca)
http://www.counterpunch.org/hribal02252010.html)

Hribal's research indicates that animal resistance is neither wild nor merely instinctive. He suggests that Descartes is wrong. Animals are making choices to defend themselves.

There is an African proverb. "Until the lion has his historian, the hunter will always be a hero."

If that is the case, then the man-killing horses presented in this study are in need of an advocate. Luckily, Sherlock Holmes had already risen to their defence.

Victims not Monsters

Once again, it is Sir Arthur Conan Doyle who provides a literary clue that casts a light on this mystery.

There were fifty-six Sherlock Holmes stories, one of which involves a racehorse, Silver Blaze, who apparently killed his trainer in cold blood. What Conan Doyle's legendary detective deduced however was that the man wasn't murdered. Holmes proved instead that while the trainer was attempting to cripple the horse with a knife, the thoroughbred kicked the man in self-preservation.

Sherlock Holmes defended Silver Blaze to his owner, explaining, "It may lessen his guilt, if I say that it was done entirely in self defence." The horse, he said, "had an instinct for intended mischief."
(*The Memoirs of Sherlock Holmes* by Sir Arthur Conan Doyle, George Newnes Co., London, 1892)

Jeremy Brett as Sherlock Holmes in the 1984 television series with "Silver Blaze"

For centuries mankind has viewed horses as commodities who cannot reason.

Perhaps instead of being horrified, we should be asking ourselves what caused horses like the Man-Killer of Lucknow to slay humans? It seems extremely unlikely that the King of England would risk the safety of his sailors, not to mention the diplomatic insult it would imply, by sending a mad and murderous horse to the Maharaja of Oude. What unknown events have never been disclosed between the time when that highly-prized, and apparently still tractable, stallion, departed from England and later, when Englishmen witnessed the animal's now terrifying actions in India? Was the horse a victim of unannounced cruelty which provoked this change in his nature? Perhaps, if the horse's sense of right and wrong has not been perceived and considered, are stories depicting him as merely a murderous savage entirely accurate? Do these lethal tales indicate that some equines refuse to be victimized, just as we would?

If so, then this might demonstrate an undetected emotional parallel between horses and humans, just as the digestive and dental similarities reveal a biological bond between our two mammalian species.

Thus, perhaps it is unfair to perceive what is under discussion as a one-dimensional horror story? What if there is undetected thread of self defence?

If so, then this leaves us with a message of light, rather than of darkness.

A Flat Earth Moment for the Equestrian World

The word "preternatural" describes something we don't have any natural explanation for right now but probably will have some day. For example, people once scoffed at the idea of magnetic attraction, because they could not explain it. Now we take it for granted.

Disclosure of the O'Reilly Anomaly could be described as a "flat-earth moment" for the horse world. You wake up with one set of beliefs but go to bed knowing your world has irrevocably changed.

As Steve McQueen stated in *The Reivers*, the film about a fish-eating racehorse, "Sometimes you have to say goodbye to the things you know and hello to the things you don't."

Such an awakening occurred in 1960 when a former secretary, turned amateur jungle researcher, made one of the most startling discoveries in recent scientific history. This came about when famed palaeontologist, Louis Leakey, assigned young Jane Goodall the task of observing a colony of chimpanzees.

The passionate naturalist set up camp in Tanzania's Gombe National Park. At that time it was commonly believed that chimpanzees were strictly vegetarian. Yet shortly after her arrival, Goodall made a stunning discovery. She witnessed the chimp colony capture, kill and eat a colobus monkey. Though she lacked collegiate training, Goodall was the first person to prove that chimps, like humans, are omnivores.

At first the established scientific community denounced Goodall's discovery, declaring that the chimpanzee behaviour uncharacteristic and the amount of meat consumed was trivial. It has since been established that a colony of predatory chimpanzees can consume nearly one ton of meat per year, routinely devouring about 150 animals per annum, including monkeys, antelopes and pigs.

Goodall's findings revolutionized the world's view of chimpanzees. Whereas they had formerly been sentimentalised, scientists realized that chimpanzees, like humans, were capable of harbouring a darker, more dangerous nature than was first suspected.

(*www.janegoodall.org/janes-first-big-discovery-chimps-eat-meat*
www-bcf.usc.edu/~stanford/chimphunt.html)

In an email to the LRG-AF, the noted anthropologist confirmed that she "has no knowledge of this kind of equine behaviour."
(*Email to LRG-AF dated 2 June, 2011*)

With the example of Goodall's chimpanzee discoveries in mind, if the world realizes that some horses are also capable of eating meat and displaying extreme aggression, then a collective readjustment could begin to occur, for it may have an unexpected impact on a surprisingly large portion of humanity.

Authors, artists, film makers, parents, neighbours, doctors, lawyers, insurance brokers and governments will have to re-examine the subject of horses in relation to their individual and collective concerns.

Nor can a furthering of this initial investigation fail to raise more academic questions. For example, when Emperor Wudi died in China 2,000 years ago, why did he choose to have his tomb guarded by 80 stallions?

(*www.horsetalk.co.nz/news/2011/02/149.shtml*)

The potential implications for a vast swathe of society are unknown.

Of even more importance to the average horse owner and rider will be the need to reassess events in their individual equestrian past. Did they experience a situation which might vindicate a previously unthinkable suspicion? Were injuries incurred that should be re-examined in a new light? Were accidents accidental or deliberate? Are they in contact with a horse whose behaviour should be reconsidered?

There are a number of new possibilities. Unfortunately, mankind is in no position to understand or investigate them.

A Future without Horses

Sceptics, who are content with their version of the equine past, will argue that because the majority are united in their belief, a single voice of objection may be ignored. These are the people who will choose to retain a tenacious loyalty to a modern myth which denies the existence of horses which are capable of killing other animals and humans. Likewise, they will scoff at the idea that horses can consume protein.

As Cassandra proved long ago, a great many people will prefer wilful blindness rather than accept the arrival of uncomfortable new facts which upset their personal belief systems.

There is however another cause for concern. If many clues are found in the past, then one of our collective dangers lies in the immediate future, where a vast majority of humanity will be more comfortable with machines than horses.

Futurists believe that by 2045 computers will have outstripped humans in terms of intelligence. These forthcoming technological changes will be so rapid and profound that experts envision a rupture in the thread of human history. The resultant influence of machines will provoke irreversible changes in humanity's course as significant as the invention of human language.

"The one thing all these theories have in common is the transformation of our species into something that is no longer recognizable as such to humanity circa 2011. This transformation has a name: the Singularity….. Maybe we'll scan our consciousness into computers and live inside them as software, forever, virtually."

(*Singularity* by Lev Grossman, Time magazine, February 21, 2011, page 21.)

Yet we don't have to look to the future to see an abundant number of clues, as many of mankind's early 20th century technical dreams have become a daily reality. The noted author and futurist, H.G. Wells, for example foresaw the internet. Sadly, he also predicted the invention of lethal machines.

The word "robot" was introduced by a Czech playwright in 1924. Since then a series of machines bearing that name have been designed to serve, answer and calculate for their human masters. They have also been programmed to kill mankind. This is demonstrated by the disclosure that there are more than 2,000 robots fighting in Afghanistan alongside the human troops.

One of the most striking developments is the invention of Big Dog, a robotic mule. Created in 2005, Big Dog is the size of a small mule and can carry more than 300 pounds of cargo. Thanks to onboard computers, the remote-controlled device, which travels at five miles an hour, can maintain its balance on ice, climb steep mountains and cross difficult terrain.

(*http://en.wikipedia.org/wiki/BigDog*
http://www.bostondynamics.com/robot_bigdog.html)

Evidence indicates that until now, robots can kill and carry. But they do not ride. They don't have that desire. They don't need to. With their lack of emotion and compassion, a machine's obsession is with efficiency. Hence it would turn to any other type of mechanized travel in preference to a horse.

In contrast, one of the unique gifts of our species is the ability to relate to other animals. A robot cannot maintain a delicate interspecies relationship as mankind does with the horse. It can analyse facts, weld cars and shoot bullets but a robot lacks the instinct to tell if a horse is off-colour.

*The Big Dog robot is a remote-controlled pack mule which can run,
climb and carry a heavy load over difficult terrain.*

Futurists share a world view based on long-term events. They have
little interest in investigating conventional equestrian wisdom. Nevertheless, though man is blessed with the ability to ride, he also has the
power to tamper with the settled order of nature.

Thus, in addition to not overlooking the future implications of these
meat-eating horses, we must endeavour not to encourage its spread.

The Danger of Unnatural Horses

As previously demonstrated, prior generations had a better overall
understanding of horses. One such scholar was R. Lee.

In the mid-nineteenth century, he reported, "Horses have not the
least objection to animal food; and it has been often given to them
when they have been obliged to perform immense journeys, or to
undergo any very great exertion. It, however, excites them very much,
and, if not judiciously bestowed, makes them fierce and uncontrollable.
Stories are told of poor men, who, when the despots of the East have
ordered them to give up their favourite horses, have fed them on flesh,
and rendered them so unmanageable, that the tyrants have no longer
desired what they once thought a prize."
(*www.gutenberg.org/ebooks/21973*)

With Lee's stern admonition in mind, there is a need to sound a note of caution in regards to intentionally feeding horses meat today.

As Historical Long Riders Sven Hedin, Gabriel Bonvalot and Frank Bessac discovered, Tibetan horses living in the hostile Himalayan mountains had limited access to grass. Therefore their owners supplemented the horses' diet by feeding them various types of meat. None of the explorers who encountered these particular animals described them as being ferocious.

Nor can it be denied that after escaping the Apaches, John Cremony revived his exhausted horse by feeding it meat. Here again, there were no stories of ill-effects.

However, these could be exceptions to the rule.

Horses have ten times our strength. They are also capable of incredible aggression, as is evidenced in numerous overlooked news stories. Several people have recently described incidents wherein their horses have been observed attacking and attempting to kill other animals, including cats, dogs, calves and skunks. One owner reported that his horse, "bit the eyeball out of a sheep, tore the ear off a ram and harassed my poor donkey almost to death."
(*http://eclectic-horseman.com/horsemanship/showthread.php?t=746*)

From Frankenstein to cloning, the idea of tampering with nature has always frightened us.

"There is a hard lesson to learn from the Greek tragedians and their poetry. At the same time, we should be grateful to Aeschylos and Euripides for demonstrating that, when the laws of nature are violated by Man, the gods respond to such hubris by rendering the animals crazy. God may forgive always, man may be forgiving from time to time, but Nature reacts harshly to every blasphemy committed by humans," warned Katerina Servi, author of *Greek Mythology*.
(*http://users.forthnet.gr/kat/antikas/Chapter28.htm*)

Recall the terrible repercussions when King Diomedes decided to feed his mares meat instead of hay. Whether the cause of the horses' madness was the flesh on which they had been fed is unknown. Yet ancient tales like these are lodged within the canon of human existence and they warn mankind that it will reap the whirlwind if it tampers with nature.

Thus, if it's wrong to deny it, it would be equally wrong to encourage it, for there may be those who will be tempted to tamper with the O'Reilly Anomaly.

Ancient and modern history proves that man hasn't changed much. When it comes to horses, competition is king and money rules the stables. That explains why Cimon of Athens fed his horses meat, in the hope that he would win the sixty-third Olympics held in 532 B.C. Likewise, George Patterson's Tibetan opponent primed his horse with spicy meat before that race in 1950.

Yet as the fictional Professor Victor Frankenstein proves, there is a danger in exploring unknown powers. People should be well aware that they are crossing into uncharted waters if they attempt to feed meat to horses.

What these stories indicate is that horses who eat flesh may gain immense strength and become fleet footed, such as Dick Turpin's mare, Black Bess. Yet it would be a mistake in today's competition-obsessed world to encourage the feeding of meat to horses, as there is no way of knowing if the animal will resemble Black Bess or the Dappled Demon.

There is instead a need for scientific analysis, as mankind tampers with nature at his own risk. This was demonstrated by the tragic episode of "mad cow disease," which also involved the unsuitability of feeding meat to certain animals. Discovered in November, 1986 Bovine Spongiform Encephalopathy is a fatal cattle disease that destroys the animal's brain and spine cord. An epidemic of BSE arose when farmers turned cattle from herbivores into cannibals, by adding ground-up cow meat and bone to their usual feed. The result was that an estimated 400,000 infected cows entered the human food chain in the 1980s.

Thus, while we can take solace in the rarity of this Anomaly, until science has investigated and defined it, tremendous care should be taken.

We should, instead, be thinking of a new way to deal with horses, one which preserves our mutual past and encourages an intellectual renaissance in the future. In order to do that, we must alter the very concept upon which horses and humans were originally bonded.

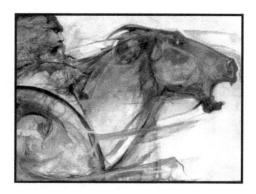

History provides ample evidence about what happens when man tampers with nature.

A New Centaur

No relationship between animals and human is more intimate, both mentally and physically, than that which exists between horse and rider, for the two share an unparalleled unity of understanding. At a time when millions of urbanized humans are denied a place in nature, the horse continues to evoke a deep emotional response. In a world full of frightening events, its benign character remains a comfort, probably because the one trait most closely associated with horses is nobility.

Yet as time has slipped away, the modern world seems to have forgotten the existence of these hidden horses who break the rules. Legends have been lost. News has been censored. Evidence has been scoffed at. All the while parables portraying horses as prey animals have become the foundation stone of a profitable new equestrian industry.

With the publication of this accumulated collection, the time has come for a re-examination of horses. Just like the majority of mankind is kind, patient, forgiving, tolerant, loving and understanding to others of his species, so is the majority of horses. Sadly, there are notable exceptions in the horse world too. Like men, there are horses who are capable of killing and harming others.

We cannot advance our unique interspecies relationship further without fully understanding the physical capabilities and emotional complexity of our equine allies. These are not meek animals. They can be hunters, predators and warriors, just like their riders. They have shaped the course of human history like no other animal has ever done before or since.

In the past, one creature embodied man's link to the horse. This was the centaur. The concept of this creature continues to have a symbolic power which remains relevant in contemporary times, especially in an era wherein humanity grows increasingly isolated from horses. However, if the centaur represents mankind's first freedom from gravity, he also presents us with an ancient warning against the irrational elements of nature.

Ancient Greeks portrayed centaurs as male creatures whose exaggerated masculinity was based upon the sexual potency of stallions. These composite creatures enjoyed a wicked reputation for being savage, drunken, violent and lustful brutes bent on destroying the laws of civilized society.

The notable exception to the centaur tradition of aggression was Chiron, as he alone was a trusted friend of mankind. This centaur taught Jason, Achilles and Odysseus to ride. He was renowned for his skills in medicine, music and archery. His was a solitary kind heart among the bestial ranks of his fellow centaurs.

As a portion of this history demonstrates, like male centaurs drunk on wine, if certain horses consume flesh, they too become violent. Yet despite the summary of fearsome facts, murderous history, and depressing news included in this study, there is a symbol of hope upon which we must conclude.

The Centaur Queen symbolizes those qualities of both species which we should strive for: intelligence, reason, kindness, patience, curiosity, courage and mutual respect. Armed with these, horses and humans can continue to explore the boundaries of the geographic and intellectual universe.

Meanwhile, as we struggle to understand the implications of the O'Reilly Anomaly, the Centaur Queen reminds us that our compassion is more compelling than our need to blame what we may not understand.

The author conceived and commissioned this image of The Centaur Queen to symbolise humanity's ancient connection to the horse. Copyright © The Long Riders' Guild.

Conclusion

We began with the ancient Greeks. Let us conclude with an even older, more benign image of humanity's prehistoric links to the horse.

Late in the evening of Sunday, December 18, 1994, a cave was discovered in southern France. Inside the previously hidden chamber, three amateur speleologists found startling evidence of Palaeolithic man's artistic nature. The walls were covered with hundreds of animal paintings, depicting at least thirteen different species. Prominent among them were many life-like drawings of Ice Age horses.
(*www.culture.gouv.fr/culture/arcnat/chauvet/en/index.html*)

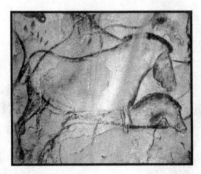

Like their modern descendants, Ice Age humans decorated the walls of their home with images of horses.

Believed to be 30,000 years old, these depictions of horses provide the earliest evidence of mankind's ongoing fascination with this special animal. Archaeologists are now trying to ascertain if the assorted images may be connected to early worship practices.

It would be easy to ridicule the beliefs of these ancestral humans, who listened to their shamans and sought comfort in animal art. Magic was a concept they used to explain what they did not understand.

Yet has man progressed so far from the core experience painted on those cave walls? Are we not still fascinated by the horse? Don't images of horses still stir our souls? Is our current equestrian wisdom so unassailable? In what way, for example, are we wiser than the Greeks? At least they discussed and wrote about King Diomedes' murderous and meat-eating horses, while the contemporary equestrian world denies their very existence.

Upon reflection, it would seem that we are more akin to our cave-dwelling ancestors than we might first realize, for like them we too are in possession of fragmentary equestrian knowledge. Luckily, we are armed with science, not magic, and can begin to deduce the meaning of this enigmatic mystery which still lurks at the edges of the known horse world.

Thus, though this book concludes, we hope it will launch an ongoing search for evidence and explanations connected to the O'Reilly Anomaly, so as to encourage the horse to be seen from a new perspective.

Scientists could undertake more research into the anomaly. Historians could institute a search for additional evidence. Trainers could acknowledge the potential dangers inherent in horses. Riding teachers could warn their pupils that horses can be more dangerous than is currently believed. Horse owners should be urged not to take chances with their safety. Finally, the public should be encouraged to alter its perception of horses, realizing that they are not necessarily passive herbivores but are instead omnivores capable of eating meat and sudden displays of savage behaviour.

The Long Riders' Guild Academic Foundation therefore extends an open invitation to readers and riders to share additional episodes, literary evidence or eyewitness accounts which help document and define the existence and behaviour of meat-eating and murderous horses.

Such information will appear in forthcoming editions of the book.

About the Author

CuChullaine O'Reilly is an investigative reporter who has spent more than thirty years studying equestrian travel techniques on every continent. After having made lengthy trips by horseback across Pakistan, he was made a Fellow of the Royal Geographical Society and the Explorers' Club. O'Reilly is also the author of *Khyber Knights*. This equestrian travel tale has been described as a "masterpiece" and the author as "Jack London in our time".

O'Reilly founded the Long Riders' Guild, the world's first international association of equestrian explorers. The organization has Members in forty-two countries, all of whom have made a qualifying equestrian journey of at least one thousand miles. The Guild has

www.lrgaf.org

supported more than a hundred equestrian expeditions on every continent except Antarctica.

The author is married to the Swiss Long Rider, Basha Cornwall-Legh, who rode her Cossack stallion, Count Pompeii, from Volgograd to London, becoming the only person in the twentieth century to ride out of Russia.

The O'Reillys are the webmasters of The Long Riders' Guild website. At three-thousand plus pages, and still growing, and having now been visited by more than three million people world-wide, this website is the repository of the largest collection of equestrian travel information in human history.

After ten years of unparalleled intellectual growth, The Long Riders' Guild became a movement for change in the wider equestrian world when the O'Reillys launched The Long Riders' Guild Academic Foundation. The world's first open-source academic equine website is devoted to the study of all hippological arts and sciences and provides a forum, free of commercial influence, wherein equine-related articles are provided at no cost to scholars, students and equine enthusiasts. Every type of horse-related knowledge is being investigated and published at this exciting website, whose motto is "Science not Superstition."

Deadly Equines is the first title in a new series of equestrian investigations undertaken by the author.

To learn more about the author, please visit these websites:
The Long Riders' Guild: www.thelongridersguild.com
The Long Riders' Guild Academic Foundation: www.lrgaf.org
Horse Travel Books: www.horsetravelbooks.com
Classic Travel Books: www.classictravelbooks.com
The World Ride: www.theworldride.org

Brown, Donald*; Journey from the Arctic* – A truly remarkable account of how Brown, his Danish companion and their two trusty horses attempt the impossible, to cross the silent Arctic plateaus, thread their way through the giant Swedish forests, and finally discover a passage around the treacherous Norwegian marshes.

Bruce, Clarence Dalrymple, *In the Hoofprints of Marco Polo* – The author made a dangerous journey from Srinagar to Peking in 1905, mounted on a trusty 13-hand Kashmiri pony, then wrote this wonderful book.

Burnaby, Frederick*; A Ride to Khiva* – Burnaby fills every page with a memorable cast of characters, including hard-riding Cossacks, nomadic Tartars, vodka-guzzling sleigh-drivers and a legion of peasant ruffians.

Burnaby, Frederick, *On Horseback through Asia Minor* – Armed with a rifle, a small stock of medicines, and a single faithful servant, the equestrian traveller rode through a hotbed of intrigue and high adventure in wild inhospitable country, encountering Kurds, Circassians, Armenians, and Persian pashas.

Carter, General William, *Horses, Saddles and Bridles* – This book covers a wide range of topics including basic training of the horse and care of its equipment. It also provides a fascinating look back into equestrian travel history.

Cayley, George, *Bridle Roads of Spain* – Truly one of the greatest equestrian travel accounts of the 19th Century.

Chase, J. Smeaton, *California Coast Trails* – This classic book describes the author's journey from Mexico to Oregon along the coast of California in the 1890s.

Chase, J. Smeaton, *California Desert Trails* – Famous British naturalist J. Smeaton Chase mounted up and rode into the Mojave Desert to undertake the longest equestrian study of its kind in modern history.

Chitty, Susan, and Hinde, Thomas, *The Great Donkey Walk* - When biographer Susan Chitty and her novelist husband, Thomas Hinde, decided it was time to embark on a family adventure, they did it in style. In Santiago they bought two donkeys whom they named Hannibal and Hamilcar. Their two small daughters, Miranda (7) and Jessica (3) were to ride Hamilcar. Hannibal, meanwhile, carried the baggage. The walk they planned to undertake was nothing short of the breadth of southern Europe.

Christian, Glynn, *Fragile Paradise: The discovery of Fletcher Christian, "Bounty" Mutineer* – the great-great-great-great-grandson of the *Bounty* mutineer brings to life a fascinating and complex character history has portrayed as both hero and villain, and the real story behind a mutiny that continues to divide opinion more than 200 years later.

Clark, Leonard, *Marching Wind, The* – The panoramic story of a mounted exploration in the remote and savage heart of Asia, a place where adventure, danger, and intrigue were the daily backdrop to wild tribesman and equestrian exploits.

Clark, Leonard, *A Wanderer Till I Die* – In a world with lax passport control, no airlines, and few rules, this young man floats effortlessly from one adventure to the next. When he's not drinking whisky at the Raffles Hotel or listening to the "St. Louis Blues" on the phonograph in the jungle, he's searching for Malaysian treasure, being captured by Toradja head-hunters, interrogated by Japanese intelligence officers and lured into shady deals by European gun-runners.

Cobbett, William, *Rural Rides, Volumes 1 and 2* – In the early 1820s Cobbett set out on horseback to make a series of personal tours through the English countryside. These books contain what many believe to be the best accounts of rural England ever written, and remain enduring classics.

Codman, John, *Winter Sketches from the Saddle* – This classic book was first published in 1888. It recommends riding for your health and describes the septuagenarian author's many equestrian journeys through New England during the winter of 1887 on his faithful mare, Fanny.

Cunninghame Graham, Jean, *Gaucho Laird* – A superbly readable biography of the author's famous great-uncle, Robert "Don Roberto" Cunninghame Graham.

Cunninghame Graham, Robert, *Horses of the Conquest* – The author uncovered manuscripts which had lain forgotten for centuries, and wrote this book, as he said, out of gratitude to the horses of Columbus and the Conquistadors who shaped history.

Cunninghame Graham, Robert, *Magreb-el-Acksa* – The thrilling tale of how "Don Roberto" was kidnapped in Morocco!

Cunninghame Graham, Robert, *Rodeo* – An omnibus of the finest work of the man they called "the uncrowned King of Scotland," edited by his friend Aimé Tschiffely.

Cunninghame Graham, Robert, *Tales of Horsemen* – Ten of the most beautifully-written equestrian stories ever set to paper.

Cunninghame Graham, Robert, *Vanished Arcadia* – This haunting story about the Jesuit missions in South America from 1550 to 1767 was the inspiration behind the best-selling film *The Mission.*

Daly, H.W., *Manual of Pack Transportation* – This book is the author's masterpiece. It contains a wealth of information on various pack saddles, ropes and equipment, how to secure every type of load imaginable and instructions on how to organize a pack train.

Dixie, Lady Florence, *Riding Across Patagonia* – When asked in 1879 why she wanted to travel to such an outlandish place as Patagonia, the author replied without hesitation that she was taking to the saddle in order to flee from the strict confines of polite Victorian society. This is the story of how the aristocrat successfully traded the perils of a London parlour for the wind-borne freedom of a wild Patagonian bronco.

Dodwell, Christina, *Beyond Siberia* – The intrepid author goes to Russia's Far East to join the reindeer-herding people in winter.

Dodwell, Christina, *An Explorer's Handbook* – The author tells you everything you want to know about travelling: how to find suitable pack animals, how to feed and shelter yourself. She also has sensible and entertaining advice about dealing with unwanted visitors and the inevitable bureaucrats.

Dodwell, Christina, *Madagascar Travels* – Christina explores the hidden corners of this amazing island and, as usual, makes friends with its people.

Dodwell, Christina, *A Traveller in China* – The author sets off alone across China, starting with a horse and then transferring to an inflatable canoe.

Dodwell, Christina, *A Traveller on Horseback* – Christina Dodwell rides through Eastern Turkey and Iran in the late 1980s. The Sunday Telegraph wrote of the author's "courage and insatiable wanderlust," and in this book she demonstrates her gift for communicating her zest for adventure.

Dodwell, Christina, *Travels in Papua New Guinea* – Christina Dodwell spends two years exploring an island little known to the outside world. She travelled by foot, horse and dugout canoe among the Stone-Age tribes.

Dodwell, Christina, *Travels with Fortune* – the truly amazing account of the courageous author's first journey – a three-year odyssey around Africa by Landrover, bus, lorry, horse, camel, and dugout canoe!

Dodwell, Christina, *Travels with Pegasus* – This time Christina takes to the air! This is the story of her unconventional journey across North Africa in a micro-light!

Downey, Bill - *Whisper on the Wind - The Story of Tom Bass, Celebrated Black Horseman* - Tom Bass rose to the summit of what had always been a white man's profession, the training of the America's greatest Saddlebred horses. An advocate of gentleness and patience, Bass turned dangerous horses into reliable mounts - without ever raising his voice or using a whip.

Duncan, John, *Travels in Western Africa in 1845 and 1846* – The author, a Lifeguardsman from Scotland, tells the hair-raising tale of his two journeys to what is now Benin. Sadly, Duncan has been forgotten until today, and we are proud to get this book back into print.

Ehlers, Otto, *Im Sattel durch die Fürstenhöfe Indiens* – In June 1890 the young German adventurer, Ehlers, lay very ill. His doctor gave him a choice: either go home to Germany or travel to Kashmir. So of course the Long Rider chose the latter. This is a thrilling yet humorous book about the author's adventures.

Farson, Negley, *Caucasian Journey* – A thrilling account of a dangerous equestrian journey made in 1929, this is an amply illustrated adventure classic.

Fox, Ernest, *Travels in Afghanistan* – The thrilling tale of a 1937 journey through the mountains, valleys, and deserts of this forbidden realm, including visits to such fabled places as the medieval city of Heart, the towering Hindu Kush mountains, and the legendary Khyber Pass.

Gall, Sandy, *Afghanistan – Agony of a Nation* - Sandy Gall has made three trips to Afghanistan to report the war there: in 1982, 1984 and again in 1986. This book is an account of his last journey and what he found. He chose to revisit the man he believes is the outstanding commander in Afghanistan: Ahmed Shah Masud, a dashing Tajik who is trying to organise resistance to the Russians on a regional, and eventually national scale.

Gall, Sandy, *Behind Russian Lines* – In the summer of 1982, Sandy Gall set off for Afghanistan on what turned out to be the hardest assignment of his life. During his career as a reporter he had covered plenty of wars and revolutions before, but this was the first time he had been required to walk all the way to an assignment and all the way back again, dodging Russian bombs *en route*.

Gallard, Babette, *Riding the Milky Way* – An essential guide to anyone planning to ride the ancient pilgrimage route to Santiago di Compostella, and a highly readable story for armchair travellers.

Galton, Francis, *The Art of Travel* – Originally published in 1855, this book became an instant classic and was used by a host of now-famous explorers, including Sir Richard Francis Burton of Mecca fame. Readers can learn how to ride horses, handle elephants, avoid cobras, pull teeth, find water in a desert, and construct a sleeping bag out of fur.

Glazier, Willard, *Ocean to Ocean on Horseback* – This book about the author's journey from New York to the Pacific in 1875 contains every kind of mounted adventure imaginable. Amply illustrated with pen and ink drawings of the time, this remains a timeless equestrian adventure classic.

Goodwin, Joseph, *Through Mexico on Horseback* – The author and his companion, Robert Horiguichi, the sophisticated, multi-lingual son of an imperial Japanese diplomat, set out in 1931 to cross Mexico. They were totally unprepared for the deserts, quicksand and brigands they were to encounter during their adventure.

Gordon, W. J., *The Horse World of Victorian London* – An enthralling and unforgettable study of the work undertaken by horses before the invention of the car.

Grant, David, *Spirit of the Vikings: A Journey in the Kayak Bahá'í Viking From Arkosund, Sweden, to Odessa, Ukraine* – David Grant takes his kayak on an adventure-filled and spiritual journey from Sweden to Odessa on the Black Sea.

Grant, David, *The Wagon Travel Handbook* - David Grant is the legendary Scottish wagon-master who journeyed around the world with his family in a horse-drawn wagon. Grant has filled The Wagon Travel Handbook with all the practical information a first time-wagon traveller will need before setting out.

Gray, David and Lukas Novotny, *Mounted Archery in the Americas* – This fascinating and amply illustrated book charts the history of mounted archery from its ancient roots on the steppes of Eurasia thousands of years ago to its current resurgence in popularity in the Americas. It also provides the reader with up-to-the-minute practical information gleaned from a unique team of the world's leading experts.

Hamilton Smith, Charles, *Equus: The Natural History of the Horse, Ass, Onager, Quagga and Zebra* - A masterpiece of erudition. The author was concerned that the public was being misled by erroneous accounts or the absence of accurate information. To rectify this error, he set about enabling equestrian essentials to emerge from obscurity, thereby authoring a book which became the principal authority on all aspects of horse-related wisdom.

Hanbury-Tenison, Marika, *For Better, For Worse* – The author, an excellent story-teller, writes about her adventures visiting and living among the Indians of Central Brazil.

Hanbury-Tenison, Marika, *A Slice of Spice* – The fresh and vivid account of the author's hazardous journey to the Indonesian Islands with her husband, Robin.

Hanbury-Tenison, Robin, *Chinese Adventure* – The story of a unique journey in which the explorer Robin Hanbury-Tenison and his wife Louella rode on horseback alongside the Great Wall of China in 1986.

Hanbury-Tenison, Robin, *Fragile Eden* – The wonderful story of Robin and Louella Hanbury-Tenison's exploration of New Zealand on horseback in 1988. They rode alone together through what they describe as 'some of the most dramatic and exciting country we have ever seen.'

Hanbury-Tenison, Robin, *Mulu: The Rainforest* – This was the first popular book to bring to the world's attention the significance of the rain forests to our fragile ecosystem. It is a timely reminder of our need to preserve them for the future.

Hanbury-Tenison, Robin, *A Pattern of Peoples* – The author and his wife, Marika, spent three months travelling through Indonesia's outer islands and writes with his usual flair and sensitivity about the tribes he found there.

Hanbury-Tenison, Robin, *A Question of Survival* – This superb book played a hugely significant role in bringing the plight of Brazil's Indians to the world's attention.

Hanbury-Tenison, Robin, *The Rough and the Smooth* – The incredible story of two journeys in South America. Neither had been attempted before, and both were considered impossible!

Hanbury-Tenison, Robin, *Spanish Pilgrimage* – Robin and Louella Hanbury-Tenison went to Santiago de Compostela in a traditional way – riding on white horses over long-forgotten tracks. In the process they discovered more about the people and the country than any conventional traveller would learn. Their adventures are vividly and entertainingly recounted in this delightful and highly readable book.

Hanbury-Tenison, Robin, *White Horses over France* – This enchanting book tells the story of a magical journey and how, in fulfilment of a personal dream, the first Camargue horses set foot on British soil in the late summer of 1984.

Hanbury-Tenison, Robin, *Worlds Apart – an Explorer's Life* – The author's battle to preserve the quality of life under threat from developers and machines infuses this autobiography with a passion and conviction which makes it impossible to put down.

Hanbury-Tenison, Robin, *Worlds Within – Reflections in the Sand* – This book is full of the adventure you would expect from a man of action like Robin Hanbury-Tenison.

However, it is also filled with the type of rare knowledge that was revealed to other desert travellers like Lawrence, Doughty and Thesiger.

Haslund, Henning, *Mongolian Adventure* – An epic tale inhabited by a cast of characters no longer present in this lacklustre world, shamans who set themselves on fire, rebel leaders who sacked towns, and wild horsemen whose ancestors conquered the world.

Hassanein, A. M., *The Lost Oases* - At the dawning of the 20th century the vast desert of Libya remained one of last unexplored places on Earth. Sir Hassanein Bey befriended the Muslim leaders of the elusive Senussi Brotherhood who controlled the deserts further on, and became aware of rumours of a "lost oasis" which lay even deeper in the desert. In 1923 the explorer led a small caravan on a remarkable seven month journey across the centre of Libya.

Heath, Frank, *Forty Million Hoofbeats* – Heath set out in 1925 to follow his dream of riding to all 48 of the Continental United States. The journey lasted more than two years, during which time Heath and his mare, Gypsy Queen, became inseparable companions.

Hinde, Thomas, *The Great Donkey Walk* – Biographer Susan Chitty and her novelist husband, Thomas Hinde, travelled from Spain's Santiago to Salonica in faraway Greece. Their two small daughters, Miranda (7) and Jessica (3) were rode one donkey, while the other donkey carried the baggage. Reading this delightful book is leisurely and continuing pleasure.

Holt, William, *Ride a White Horse* – After rescuing a cart horse, Trigger, from slaughter and nursing him back to health, the 67-year-old Holt and his horse set out in 1964 on an incredible 9,000 mile, non-stop journey through western Europe.

Hope, Thomas, *Anastasius* – Here is the book that took the world by storm, and then was forgotten. Hope's hero Anastasius was fearless, curious, cunning, ruthless, brave, and above all, sexy. He journeyed deep into the vast and dangerous Ottoman Empire. During the 35 years described in the book (1762-1798) the swashbuckling hero infiltrated the deadly Wahhabis in Arabia, rode to war with the Mamelukes in Egypt and sailed the Mediterranean with the Turks. This remarkable new edition features all three volumes together for the first time.

Hopkins, Frank T., *Hidalgo and Other Stories* – For the first time in history, here are the collected writings of Frank T. Hopkins, the counterfeit cowboy whose endurance racing claims and Old West fantasies have polarized the equestrian world.

Jacobs, Ross, *Old Men and Horses – A Gift of Horsemanship* - Ross Jacobs is an extraordinary and experienced Australian horseman, trainer and writer. In *Old Men and Horses* he has created three fictional characters whose role in the history of equestrian training will never be forgotten.

James, Jeremy, *Saddletramp* – The classic story of Jeremy James' journey from Turkey to Wales, on an unplanned route with an inaccurate compass, unreadable map and the unfailing aid of villagers who seemed to have as little sense of direction as he had.

James, Jeremy, *Vagabond* – The wonderful tale of the author's journey from Bulgaria to Berlin offers a refreshing, witty and often surprising view of Eastern Europe and the collapse of communism.

Jebb, Louisa, *By Desert Ways to Baghdad and Damascus* – From the pen of a gifted writer and intrepid traveller, this is one of the greatest equestrian travel books of all time.

Kluckhohn, Clyde, *To the Foot of the Rainbow* – This is not just a exciting true tale of equestrian adventure. It is a moving account of a young man's search for physical perfection in a desert world still untouched by the recently-born twentieth century.

Lambie, Thomas, *Boots and Saddles in Africa* – Lambie's story of his equestrian journeys is told with the grit and realism that marks a true classic.

Landor, Henry Savage, *In the Forbidden Land* – Illustrated with hundreds of photographs and drawings, this blood-chilling account of equestrian adventure makes for page-turning excitement.

Langlet, Valdemar, *Till Häst Genom Ryssland (Swedish)* – Denna reseskildring rymmer många ögonblicksbilder av möten med människor, från morgonbad med Lev Tolstoi till samtal med Tartarer och fotografering av fagra skördeflickor. Rikt illustrerad med foto och teckningar.

Leigh, Margaret, *My Kingdom for a Horse* – In the autumn of 1939 the author rode from Cornwall to Scotland, resulting in one of the most delightful equestrian journeys of the early twentieth century. This book is full of keen observations of a rural England that no longer exists.

Lester, Mary, *A Lady's Ride across Spanish Honduras in 1881* – This is a gem of a book, with a very entertaining account of Mary's vivid, day-to-day life in the saddle.

MacDermot, Brian, *Cult of the Sacred Spear* – here is that rarest of travel books, an exploration not only of a distant land but of a man's own heart. A confederation of pastoral people located in Southern Sudan and western Ethiopia, the Nuer warriors were famous for staging cattle raids against larger tribes and successfully resisted European colonization. Brian MacDermot, London stockbroker, entered into Nuer society as a stranger and emerged as Rial Nyang, an adopted member of the tribe. This book recounts this extraordinary emotional journey

Maeterlinck, Maurice, *Clever Hans and the Elberfeld Horses* – In the early 20th Century, a German stallion named Clever Hans could apparently communicate with humans. The discovery of this remarkable animal, who could supposedly also spell and tell time, caused such an uproar that the German government appointed the "Hans Commission" to investigate the astonishing claims. The Commission concluded in September, 1904 that no tricks were involved. A sceptical psychologist however declared that the horse's owner was guilty of inadvertently signalling the answers to Hans. The mystery remains: can horses communicate with humans?

Maillart, Ella, *Turkestan Solo* – A vivid account of a 1930s journey through this wonderful, mysterious and dangerous portion of the world, complete with its Kirghiz eagle hunters, lurking Soviet secret police, and the timeless nomads that still inhabited the desolate steppes of Central Asia.

Marcy, Randolph, *The Prairie Traveler* – There were a lot of things you packed into your saddlebags or the wagon before setting off to cross the North American wilderness in the 1850s. A gun and an axe were obvious necessities. Yet many pioneers were just as adamant about placing a copy of Captain Randolph Marcy's classic book close at hand.

Marsden, Kate, *Riding through Siberia: A Mounted Medical Mission in 1891* – This immensely readable book is a mixture of adventure, extreme hardship and compassion as the author travels the Great Siberian Post Road.

Marsh, Hippisley Cunliffe, *A Ride Through Islam* – A British officer rides through Persia and Afghanistan to India in 1873. Full of adventures, and with observant remarks on the local Turkoman equestrian traditions.

MacCann, William, *Viaje a Caballo* – Spanish-language edition of the British author's equestrian journey around Argentina in 1848.

Mason, Theodore, *The South Pole Ponies* – The touching and totally forgotten story of the little horses who gave their all to both Scott and Shackleton in their attempts to reach the South Pole.

Meline, James, *Two Thousand Miles on Horseback: Kansas to Santa Fé in 1866* – A beautifully written, eye witness account of a United States that is no more.

Muir Watson, Sharon, *The Colour of Courage* – The remarkable true story of the epic horse trip made by the first people to travel Australia's then-unmarked Bicentennial National Trail. There are enough adventures here to satisfy even the most jaded reader.

Naysmith, Gordon, *The Will to Win* – This book recounts the only equestrian journey of its kind undertaken during the 20th century - a mounted trip stretching across 16 countries. Gordon Naysmith, a Scottish pentathlete and former military man, set out in 1970 to ride from the tip of the African continent to the 1972 Olympic Games in distant Germany.

Ondaatje, Christopher, *Leopard in the Afternoon* – The captivating story of a journey through some of Africa's most spectacular haunts. It is also touched with poignancy and regret for a vanishing wilderness – a world threatened with extinction.

Ondaatje, Christopher, *The Man-Eater of Pununai* – a fascinating story of a past rediscovered through a remarkable journey to one of the most exotic countries in the world — Sri Lanka. Full of drama and history, it not only relives the incredible story of a man-eating leopard that terrorized the tiny village of Punanai in the early part of the century, but also allows the author to come to terms with the ghost of his charismatic but tyrannical father.

Ondaatje, Christopher, *Sindh Revisited* – This is the extraordinarily sensitive account of the author's quest to uncover the secrets of the seven years Richard Burton spent in India in the army of the East India Company from 1842 to 1849. "If I wanted to fill the gap in my understanding of Richard Burton, I would have to do something that had never been done before: follow in his footsteps in India…" The journey covered thousands of miles—trekking across deserts where ancient tribes meet modern civilization in the valley of the mighty Indus River.

O'Connor, Derek, *The King's Stranger* – a superb biography of the forgotten Scottish explorer, John Duncan.

O'Reilly, Basha, *Count Pompeii – Stallion of the Steppes* – the story of Basha's journey from Russia with her stallion, Count Pompeii, told for children. This is the first book in the *Little Long Rider* series.

O'Reilly, CuChullaine, (Editor) *The Horse Travel Handbook* – this accumulated knowledge of a million miles in the saddle tells you everything you need to know about travelling with your horse!

O'Reilly, CuChullaine, (Editor) *The Horse Travel Journal* – a unique book to take on your ride and record your experiences. Includes the world's first equestrian travel "pictionary" to help you in foreign countries.

O'Reilly, CuChullaine, *Khyber Knights* – Told with grit and realism by one of the world's foremost equestrian explorers, "Khyber Knights" has been penned the way lives are lived, not how books are written.

O'Reilly, CuChullaine, (Editor) *The Long Riders, Volume One* – The first of five unforgettable volumes of exhilarating travel tales.

Östrup, J, (Swedish), *Växlande Horisont* – The thrilling account of the author's journey to Central Asia from 1891 to 1893.

Patterson, George, *Gods and Guerrillas* – The true and gripping story of how the author went secretly into Tibet to film the Chinese invaders of his adopted country. Will make your heart pound with excitement!

Patterson, George, *Journey with Loshay: A Tibetan Odyssey* – This is an amazing book written by a truly remarkable man! Relying both on his companionship with God and on his own strength, he undertook a life few can have known, and a journey of emergency across the wildest parts of Tibet.

Patterson, George, *Patterson of Tibet* – Patterson was a Scottish medical missionary who went to Tibet shortly after the second World War. There he became Tibetan in all but name, adapting to the culture and learning the language fluently. This intense autobiography reveals how Patterson crossed swords with India's Prime Minister Nehru, helped with the rescue of the Dalai Lama and befriended a host of unique world figures ranging from Yehudi Menhuin to Eric Clapton. This is a vividly-written account of a life of high adventure and spiritual odyssey.

Pocock, Roger, *Following the Frontier* – Pocock was one of the nineteenth century's most influential equestrian travellers. Within the covers of this book is the detailed account of Pocock's horse ride along the infamous Outlaw Trail, a 3,000 mile solo journey that took the adventurer from Canada to Mexico City.

Pocock, Roger, *Horses* – Pocock set out to document the wisdom of the late 19th and early 20th Centuries into a book unique for its time. His concerns for attempting to preserve equestrian knowledge were based on cruel reality. More than 300,000 horses had been destroyed during the recent Boer War. Though Pocock enjoyed a reputation for dangerous living, his observations on horses were praised by the leading thinkers of his day.

Post, Charles Johnson, *Horse Packing* – Originally published in 1914, this book was an instant success, incorporating as it did the very essence of the science of packing horses and mules. It makes fascinating reading for students of the horse or history.

Ray, G. W., *Through Five Republics on Horseback* – In 1889 a British explorer – part-time missionary and full-time adventure junky – set out to find a lost tribe of sun-worshipping natives in the unexplored forests of Paraguay. The journey was so brutal that it defies belief.

Rink, Bjarke, *The Centaur Legacy* – This immensely entertaining and historically important book provides the first ever in-depth study into how man's partnership with his equine companion changed the course of history and accelerated human development.

Ross, Julian, *Travels in an Unknown Country* – A delightful book about modern horseback travel in an enchanting country, which once marked the eastern borders of the Roman Empire – Romania.

Ross, Martin and Somerville, E, *Beggars on Horseback* – The hilarious adventures of two aristocratic Irish cousins on an 1894 riding tour of Wales.

Ruxton, George, *Adventures in Mexico* – The story of a young British army officer who rode from Vera Cruz to Santa Fe, Mexico in 1847. At times the author exhibits a fearlessness which borders on insanity. He ignores dire warnings, rides through deadly deserts, and dares murderers to attack him. It is a delightful and invigorating tale of a time and place now long gone.

von Salzman, Erich, *Im Sattel durch Zentralasien* – The astonishing tale of the author's journey through China, Turkestan and back to his home in Germany – 6000 kilometres in 176 days!

Schwarz, Hans *(German)*, *Vier Pferde, Ein Hund und Drei Soldaten* – In the early 1930s the author and his two companions rode through Liechtenstein, Austria, Romania, Albania, Yugoslavia, to Turkey, then rode back again!

Schwarz, Otto *(German)*, *Reisen mit dem Pferd* – the Swiss Long Rider with more miles in the saddle than anyone else tells his wonderful story, and a long appendix tells the reader how to follow in his footsteps.

Scott, Robert, *Scott's Last Expedition* – Many people are unaware that Scott recruited Yakut ponies from Siberia for his doomed expedition to the South Pole in 1909. Here is the remarkable story of men and horses who all paid the ultimate sacrifice.

Shackleton, Ernest, *Aurora Australis* - The members of the British Antarctic Expedition of 1907-1908 wrote this delightful and surprisingly funny book. It was printed on the spot "at the sign of the Penguin"!

Skrede, Wilfred, *Across the Roof of the World* – This epic equestrian travel tale of a wartime journey across Russia, China, Turkestan and India is laced with unforgettable excitement.

Stevens, Thomas, *Through Russia on a Mustang* – Mounted on his faithful horse, Texas, Stevens crossed the Steppes in search of adventure. Cantering across the pages of this classic tale is a cast of nineteenth century Russian misfits, peasants, aristocrats— and even famed Cossack Long Rider Dmitri Peshkov.

Stevenson, Robert L., *Travels with a Donkey* – In 1878, the author set out to explore the remote Cevennes mountains of France. He travelled alone, unless you count his stubborn and manipulative pack-donkey, Modestine. This book is a true classic.

Strong, Anna Louise, *Road to the Grey Pamir* – With Stalin's encouragement, Strong rode into the seldom-seen Pamir mountains of faraway Tajikistan. The political renegade turned equestrian explorer soon discovered more adventure than she had anticipated.

Sykes, Ella, *Through Persia on a Sidesaddle* – Ella Sykes rode side-saddle 2,000 miles across Persia, a country few European woman had ever visited. Mind you, she travelled in style, accompanied by her Swiss maid and 50 camels loaded with china, crystal, linens and fine wine.

Trinkler, Emile, *Through the Heart of Afghanistan* – In the early 1920s the author made a legendary trip across a country now recalled only in legends.

Tschiffely, Aimé, *Bohemia Junction* – "Forty years of adventurous living condensed into one book."

Tschiffely, Aimé, *Bridle Paths* – a final poetic look at a now-vanished Britain.

Tschiffely, Aimé, *Coricancha*: A fascinating and balanced account of the conquest of the Inca Empire.

Tschiffely, Aimé, *Don Roberto* – A biography of Tschiffely's friend and mentor, Robert Cunninghame Graham.

Tschiffely, Aimé, *Little Princess Turtle Dove* – An enchanting fairy story set in South America and displaying Aimé Tschiffely's love, not only for children and animals, but also for South America.

Tschiffely, Aimé, *Mancha y Gato Cuentan sus Aventuras* – The Spanish-language version of *The Tale of Two Horses* – the story of the author's famous journey as told by the horses.

Tschiffely, Aimé, *Ming and Ping*: An adventure book for older children. The title characters go exploring South America together. They meet many tribes of Indians and learn about their way of life. Exhilarating and effortlessly instructive.

Tschiffely, Aimé, *Round and About Spain:* Tschiffely sets off to explore Spain, but this time his steed is a motorbike, not a horse! With wit, wisdom and a sharp eye for the absurd, he travels to all four corners of this fascinating country and makes many friends along the way. So much has changed since the Second World War that that this book is a unique snapshot of Spain as she was in 1950.

Tschiffely, Aimé, *The Tale of Two Horses* – The story of Tschiffely's famous journey from Buenos Aires to Washington, DC, narrated by his two equine heroes, Mancha and Gato. Their unique point of view is guaranteed to delight children and adults alike.

Tschiffely, Aimé, *This Way Southward* – the most famous equestrian explorer of the twentieth century decides to make a perilous journey across the U-boat infested Atlantic.

Tschiffely, Aimé, *Tschiffely's Ride* – The true story of the most famous equestrian journey of the twentieth century – 10,000 miles with two Criollo geldings from Argentina to Washington, DC. A new edition is coming soon with a Foreword by his literary heir!

Tschiffely, Aimé, *Tschiffely's Ritt* – The German-language translation of *Tschiffely's Ride* – the most famous equestrian journey of its day.

Ure, John, *Cucumber Sandwiches in the Andes* – No-one who wasn't mad as a hatter would try to take a horse across the Andes by one of the highest passes between Chile and the Argentine. That was what John Ure was told on his way to the British Embassy in Santiago – so he set out to find a few certifiable kindred spirits. Fans of equestrian travel and of Latin America will be enchanted by this delightful book.

Walker, Elaine, *To Amaze the People with Pleasure and Delight: the horsemanship manuals of William Cavendish, Duke of Newcastle* - One cannot study mankind's attempts to understand and train, the horse without considering the remarkable career of English horseman, William Cavendish, the Duke of Newcastle. In 1658 Newcastle authored one of the world's most enlightened books on equestrian training. British writer and Newcastle scholar, Dr. Elaine Walker, has undertaken an in-depth study of the Duke's horsemanship manuals, considering them as key texts in the history of the relationship between humans and the horse.

Warner, Charles Dudley, *On Horseback in Virginia* – A prolific author, and a great friend of Mark Twain, Warner made witty and perceptive contributions to the world of nineteenth century American literature. This book about the author's equestrian adventures is full of fascinating descriptions of nineteenth century America.

Weale, Magdalene, *Through the Highlands of Shropshire* – It was 1933 and Magdalene Weale was faced with a dilemma: how to best explore her beloved English countryside? By horse, of course! This enchanting book invokes a gentle, softer world inhabited by gracious country lairds, wise farmers, and jolly inn keepers.

Weeks, Edwin Lord, *Artist Explorer* – A young American artist and superb writer travels through Persia to India in 1892.

Wentworth Day, J., *Wartime Ride* – In 1939 the author decided the time was right for an extended horseback ride through England! While parts of his country were being ravaged by war, Wentworth Day discovered an inland oasis of mellow harvest fields, moated Tudor farmhouses, peaceful country halls, and fishing villages.

Von Westarp, Eberhard, *Unter Halbmond und Sonne* – (German) – Im Sattel durch die asiatische Türkei und Persien.

Wilkins, Messanie, *Last of the Saddle Tramps* – Told she had little time left to live, the author decided to ride from her native Maine to the Pacific. Accompanied by her faithful horse, Tarzan, Wilkins suffered through any number of obstacles, including blistering deserts and freezing snow storms – and defied the doctors by living for another 20 years!

Wilson, Andrew, *The Abode of Snow* – One of the best accounts of overland equestrian travel ever written about the wild lands that lie between Tibet and Afghanistan.

de Windt, Harry, *A Ride to India* – Part science, all adventure, this book takes the reader for a thrilling canter across the Persian Empire of the 1890s.

Winthrop, Theodore, *Saddle and Canoe* – This book paints a vibrant picture of 1850s life in the Pacific Northwest and covers the author's travels along the Straits of Juan De Fuca, on Vancouver Island, across the Naches Pass, and on to The Dalles, in Oregon Territory. This is truly an historic travel account.

Woolf, Leonard, *Stories of the East* – Three short stories which are of vital importance in understanding the author's mistrust of and dislike for colonialism, which provide disturbing commentaries about the disintegration of the colonial process.
Younghusband, George, *Eighteen Hundred Miles on a Burmese Pony* – One of the funniest and most enchanting books about equestrian travel of the nineteenth century, featuring "Joe" the naughty Burmese pony!

We are constantly adding new titles to our collections, so please check our websites:

www.horsetravelbooks.com - www.classictravelbooks.com

The Equestrian Wisdom & History Series: www.lrgaf.org